*The Art of* SERIES
EDITED BY CHARLES BAXTER

*The Art of* series is a line of books reinvigorating the practice of craft and criticism. Each book is a brief, witty, and useful exploration of fiction, nonfiction, or poetry by a writer impassioned by a singular craft issue. *The Art of* volumes provide a series of sustained examinations of key, but sometimes neglected, aspects of creative writing by some of contemporary literature's finest practitioners.

# THE ART OF SYNTAX

## RHYTHM OF THOUGHT, RHYTHM OF SONG

*Other Books by Ellen Bryant Voigt*

*The Art of*

# SYNTAX

**RHYTHM OF THOUGHT,
RHYTHM OF SONG**

*Ellen Bryant Voigt*

Graywolf Press

Publication of this volume is made possible in part by a grant provided by the Minnesota State Arts Board, through an appropriation by the Minnesota State Legislature; a grant from the Wells Fargo Foundation Minnesota; and a grant from the National Endowment for the Arts, which believes that a great nation deserves great art. Significant support has also been provided by the Bush Foundation; Target; the McKnight Foundation; and other generous contributions from foundations, corporations, and individuals. To these organizations and individuals we offer our heartfelt thanks.

This book is made possible through a partnership with the College of Saint Benedict, and honors the legacy of S. Mariella Gable, a distinguished teacher at the College. Support has been provided by the Lee and Rose Warner Foundation as part of the Warner Reading Program.

Published by Graywolf Press
212 Third Avenue North, Suite 485
Minneapolis, Minnesota 55401
All rights reserved.

www.graywolfpress.org

Published in the United States of America

ISBN 978-1-55597-531-9

10  12  14  16  15  13  11  9

Library of Congress Control Number: 2008941981

Series cover design: Scott Sorenson

Cover art: Scott Sorenson

*for Stephen Dobyns*

# Contents

# Preface

The summer I turned nineteen, I had a job in a restaurant known for its "singing waiters and waitresses." We were all conservatory refugees, trying to earn next year's tuition, and I was the piano player. Mainly, I was Shopping Mall Music—show tunes, jazz standards, Old Favorites like "Clair de Lune" or Pachabel, to soften the ticket price for prime rib. Every day, two hours at lunch and from five until closing, I noodled around familiar melodies, put together medleys ("Moonlight in Vermont" to "Moon River" to "Lazy River"), or stylized requests. My first triumph came late one night when a large table, very loud and very jolly, requested "The Sheik of Araby." I'd never heard of it, nor was the song to be found in the fat, frayed Fake Book I consulted discreetly in the ladies' room. So I rode the long vowels in C minor ("Oh—the SHEEK-*and-2-and-3*, of Ar-a-BEE-*and-2-and-3*), repeated the phrase in several other keys, tossed in a showy glissando, and pocketed a fifty-dollar tip. They were deep in their cups.

My public trial by saturation also involved another sort of ear training. Periodically, a waitress would put down her tray and prop "The Man I Love" or Puccini on the rack of the grand ("Transpose this down a third," she might say without a wink). There was never time to rehearse—ketchup bottles and salt shakers needed filling between shifts—and "Un bel di" might not have been in your repertoire at age nineteen, any more than "The Sheik of Araby." Like skydiving or high-stakes poker, with sight reading—the first sighting of the thing—you're playing the odds, relying as much on your ear as on your eye, and, crucially, on a prior knowledge of patterns.

Ear training is learning how to duplicate both any sound you hear and any as-yet-unheard sound indicated on the score. Perfect pitch is only a small advantage—what matters more is *relative* pitch, the intervals between notes, so one's instinctive aim is true. For an accompanist, there's even more to calibrate—rhythm and harmony, for instance, since you are the whole orchestra. Confronting an unfamiliar score, the eye needs to zoom ahead, using the current sound to predict the next cluster of sounds, locating markers of confirmation or redirection; the fingers simply follow with their split-second translation. It only works if you can narrow the range of choices at each given moment. This means you need to have already tutored the instincts that now must leap into action—to have *already learned* what chords are encompassed by any given key and their most likely sequence.

Being overheard, and the relentless ongoing pulse, are large and stressful differences, but in fact, reading anything at all employs the same brain work, the same rapid-fire reliance on deeply learned patterns, which are either fulfilled or resisted. When what we read is written not in musical notation but in words, those patterns are embedded in the syntax of the language. Writers who employ them with wit and surprise, with satisfying musical structure, with clarity of purpose and subtlety of meaning, provide us one of the greatest satisfactions of the literary arts. And the art most attentive to pattern of every kind is poetry.

The following pages investigate some of the ways a poet composes with and against and inside the syntactical patterns available in English. The opening chapter identifies the most common patterns and their musical arrangement in passages from Robert Frost and Maeve Brennan. Chapter 2 examines, in free verse poems by Stanley Kunitz and D. H. Lawrence, how choices for meaning and music multiply exponentially when a poetic line, with its own myriad choices, either reinforces or complicates the sentence. In chapter 3, Shakespeare's Sonnet 29 dramatizes the powerful balance of meter and phrase, and the next three chapters track the way phrase destabilizes meter in Philip Larkin, structures the relaxed accentual verse of Elizabeth Bishop, and propels the syllabic lines of Donald Justice. Completing the circle, the final chapter returns to Lawrence, free verse, and syntactical patterns that score a narrative.

One of my touchstones throughout is Robert Frost, who had some sly and pithy things to say about these matters, and I recommend going directly to the source. Another touchstone is Robert Jourdain, whose analysis of music, using analogs borrowed from linguistics, provided helpful lenses for poetry, which incorporates both fields. For more about language acquisition, Steven Pinker provides an excellent introduction. And at the back of this book there is a glossary of the terms I use to talk concretely about meter and phrase, line and syntax—names for the parts. With poetry as with music, the first step toward mastery is recognition.

# THE ART OF SYNTAX

### RHYTHM OF THOUGHT,
### RHYTHM OF SONG

# Language, Literacy, and Literature

The best time to visit doting literate parents and their firstborn is between years one and two. They won't ask you to change the diaper, and you'll see confirmed the two seminal theories of language acquisition: Jean Piaget's tabula rasa, the child imprinted by example and instruction; and Noam Chomsky's hardwired "generative" or "transformational" grammar.

Piaget explains best the accrual of a lexicon, one's individual stash of words. This usually begins as idiosyncratic sounds the fond parent will push toward semantic meaning; drawing on the context and a deep belief in the genius of his offspring, he translates these sounds into names—of objects, people, actions, even abstractions. When I saw Emily at eighteen months, she was pointing out purple, yellow, and red; in a few more months, as the child of poets she probably added mauve, chartreuse, and ecru. Similarly, Emily could already count up to three blocks or books or velvet bears, "one," "two," and "three" not just parroted and memorized sounds but specific denotations she knew and could apply.

More recently (Fond Parent has reported), after counting out three of the beans on her plate, Emily burst into a little aria: "fourfivesixseveneight." She doesn't actually *count* that high: the string of sounds belongs not yet to meaningful speech but to song, an aspect of language development predicted by Chomsky and confirmed in recent studies of the brain. First learned, last lost, musical strings like Emily's advanced numbers will often survive brain injury or deterioration that blocks the usual access to the lexicon. A stroke victim may be able to recover specific time reference, such as "last Tuesday," only by first reciting MondayTuesdayWednesdayThursday FridaySaturdaySunday—the organizing chunk it belongs to, which is also how I retrieve, after years of disuse, the days of the week in French. "Chunking" is a normal and widespread brain function, essential to what we think of as human intelligence and to memory. The construction 78-321-78 does not declare itself as a telephone number but 783-2178 does, if you're American; Europeans expect numbers grouped in pairs (country code, city code, etc.); your Social Security number—xxx-xx-xxxx—is its own little rhythmic motif.

The refrains of a child are not only learned, like the preceding examples, but are sometimes purely self-generated. One of Emily's private codes is "nu-nu-nu-nu-nu," which she uses when she wants to nurse. Toddlers are full of such ejaculation and imperative, and each time they are flirting with a rudimentary sentence, Chomsky's "deep structure." Each time, too, attentive parents will push the sound toward full syntax, and thereby communicable meaning, with a variety of more elaborate "surface structures": "Do you want to nurse now, Emily?" or "After you finish your beans you can nurse." She learns these syntactical arrangements indirectly, as song, like so much of the incomprehensible adult speech she overhears—strings of vowels and consonants, syllables that comprise words, and strings of words themselves arranged in (to us) meaningful relation to one another. The common surface structures we use are too numerous, too various, to be simply memorized as words are. Instead, Emily is absorbing the rules of the local game she was born to play.

And the game grows increasingly complex, to include varieties of tone and context. In a few years, she'll have down pat the formal arrangement of a joke. "Knock knock," says the six-year-old. "Who's there?" replies the willing partner. "Banana." "Banana who?" "Banana and Salami. Ha-ha-ha-ha." Semantic meaning will arrive later; meanwhile, her joke demonstrates musical meaning, significance attributable to—derivative of—form, which is to say pattern, a replicable arrangement of parts.

In the rapid acquisition of language, nature (Chomsky's view) does not stand opposed to nurture (Piaget's view)—there is constant interplay between them. Each formative, evolved human brain, Chomsky says, arrives equipped for any coherent language system. Between six and twenty-four months, the many latent possibilities begin closing off in favor of specialization, facility with the particular language or languages at hand. A baby hearing only Thai loses the inherent ability to distinguish automatically between an "L" sound and an "R"; Russians speaking English often overlook articles, which don't pertain in their native tongue; and although French children have no trouble with gendered nouns, I once entered a fancy cheese shop in Provence and asked for "*la* chevre"—the goat. In each case, the primary language had efficiently monopolized areas in those brains for its own favorite set of LEGOs, with which myriad houses and towers and bridges are erected.

In English, the fundamental building blocks are subject, verb, and optional verb object. The fundament is so crucial, we use it to define our most powerful and coherent structure—the sentence. To say, as most dictionaries and grammar books do, that a sentence provides a complete thought is actually to say it resolves the brain's search for the fundament. That is, every complete English sentence contains both a subject (a noun or pronoun that does or receives an action or simply is) and a predicate (a verb, which specifies that action or existence). Whether or not this fundament is amplified with other chunks of linguistic information (modifiers, they are called), its presence alone creates a clause. If nothing subordinates—makes incomplete—that clause (such as *before, after, while, when,* or *if, which, because, unless*), it is therefore "independent" and creates a sentence, a unit of thought. Primers are full of this most rudimentary form of sentence.

But even if young children cannot read them yet, they certainly do comprehend far more complex grammatical arrangements when they hear them. "After you finish your beans" has a subject and a predicate, but "after" has tagged that clause as subordinate, incomplete; even a toddler's brain does not mistake it for the "main idea"—"[then] you can nurse." She can also process the other version of that sentence, which changes the structural relationship—the power relationship—between the independent and dependent (subordinate) clauses: "Before you can nurse, you must finish your beans." Years of psychotherapy have been spent in response to such differences.

The fundament, then, is the crucial unit of coherence and relation. Grammar controls the function of each word in the sentence and lines it up on one side of a clause or the other: "mask" can be a thing (noun) or an action (verb), depending on its usage. Grammar also regulates that usage, and the lexicon, to efficiently signal function (*he* or *him; laugh* or *laughs*). These are tactics for clarity of discursive (paraphrasable) information.

Syntax, however, is a larger, more flexible calculus: the order of the words in each unique human utterance. It is a strategy, an arrangement of constituent parts, the manner in which the fundament and its dependent adjuncts, large or small, are deployed.

Neurolinguists now have at their disposal increasingly sophisticated equipment for mapping the brain as it processes language, and have discovered that the two quite distinct kinds of language development—acquiring a lexicon and mastering syntax—occur in different areas. An MRI would light up one of these when Emily names her beans "one," "two," and "three," another when she sings out the remaining numbers or tells her rudimentary joke. And these syntax centers are not only independent from word deposits but adjacent to where we process music.

Music has been fairly defined as organized sound: identifiable elements recur over time. Its hallmark is sufficiently recognizable patterns causing a brain to repeatedly group notes in the same way, according to Robert Jourdain in *Music, the Brain, and Ecstasy.* That is, it sorts and arranges perception. Organized sound may also fairly define speech. Routinely, analysis of music employs linguistic terms—phrase, meaning, idea—because "our brains treat musical phrases and spoken phrases similarly, suspending comprehension as a phrase arrives, then pausing to gulp the whole thing down." This "chunking" is the essential work of syntax, and it is how we make meaning: from a rudimentary set of principles (Chomsky's requisite deep structure), we generate or interpret surface structures of infinite variety that combine, in parsable sequence, words from our acquired lexicons. After years of exposure to hundreds of thousands of these surface structures, each bearing its own direct and/or trace connections to the English fundament of subject-verb-(object), we can, like Fond Parent, expect a grown-up Emily to understand— perhaps even compose—something like this:

> Back out of all this now too much for us,
> Back in a time made simple by the loss
> Of detail, burned, dissolved, and broken off
> Like graveyard marble sculpture in the weather,
> There is a house that is no more a house
> Upon a farm that is no more a farm
> And in a town that is no more a town.

The first sentence of Robert Frost's "Directive" depends on the same deep structure evoked by the toddler's partial utterance even as it uses longer musical phrases in a more complex relation to one another. Syntax identifies the order in which these strings or chains or chunks of language appear. When the chunks differ in relative weight and grammatical importance, as they do here, the surface structure is hypotactic. That is, the sentence contains more than one clause, but at least one of them is more powerful than the others, controlling everything with *its* independent subject and predicate. (As a reminder of the deep structure underlying our language, I will call that essential chunk of syntax "the fundament" throughout this book.) Hypotaxis names one of the kinds of common surface structures we routinely recognize in English. It is a characteristic rhythm of adult thought, processed by listening or reading brains as they would a Brahms concerto.

While neurolinguistics has provided a useful tool for musicology, music is in turn a helpful analog for any consideration of artistic language use. Phrasing in music, Jourdain reminds us, "is nothing like [musical] meter. For one thing, its markers are more subtle. Where meter presents a regular, mostly predictable succession of emphasized notes, phrasing constantly varies." Dynamics, harmony, melodic line, variations in rhythm—all can be "markers" in music, notifying the listener where phrases begin and end, enabling a "series of distinct musical shapes extending across time." Rhythmic markers in particular "cut up a torrent of notes into bite-size chunks," with small chunks then grouped into larger chunks, to enable "our perception of complex hierarchies."

Syntax supplies language most of its similar markers, and we've known many of them since childhood. A period marks a sentence as a discrete structure, composed primarily of moveable parts or chunks (noun phrase, verb phrase, etc.) that are processed by the brain sequentially. As soon as a group of words makes tentative sense, we file it away temporarily, according to its relationship to the fundament, and look for the next one. In language as in music, repetition— whether lexical (the same words) or grammatical (the same function for the words) or syntactical (the same arrangement of the words)—also marks phrases or chunks. As in music, these units can also be grouped into even larger chunks, paragraphs or stanzas, to form astonishingly elaborate but comprehensible structures.

In Frost's opening lines, pentameter and anaphora (repeated head of the line) are clear markers *(Back . . . , Back),* reinforced by the cleverly opposed prepositions *(Back **out** . . . Back **in** . . .).* Other markers are implied by parallel function. *Burned, dissolved, and broken off,* three past participles, attached to the same noun, contain trace elements of elided clauses: [which was] burned, [which was] dissolved, [which was] broken off. The human brain is avid for pattern, by which to register, store, and retrieve information—and parallelism is one of the more common patterns in English syntax. It is also the most democratic. With parallelism, we are given pieces of information of equal syntactical importance, whether these chunks are clauses, organizing the sentence, or only modifiers, structurally unnecessary but crucial to precision *(Like graveyard marble sculpture in the weather).*

Another predictable recurrence is instead hierarchical, like those diagrammed sentences in eighth grade that threatened to wander off the right edge of the blackboard and onto the wall. In the syntactical pattern known as right-branching, modification follows in closest proximity to what it modifies; the listener or reader is not taxed to remember or anticipate the referent. This is one way to compensate in English for the lack of inflected word endings, which specifically indicate certain grammatical functions (we spell them out instead with function words, like prepositions). In the "language tree" linguists like to invoke, the trunk of the fundament branches off into limbs, which subdivide again and again into more limbs and, finally, twigs. In syntax that is right-branching (the linear direction of English), each new "chunk" is directly attached to, even seems to grow out of, what immediately preceded it:

Back in a time (which time?)
    a time made simple (made simple how?)
        made simple by the loss (what kind of loss?)
            the loss of detail (what kind of detail?)

detail burned, dissolved, and broken off
(how broken off?)
like graveyard marble sculpture in
the weather.

Frost is a master of branching syntax, the chunks reinforced by the poem's lines—this is one way he approximates speech. Right-branching, like parallelism, allows the elision of function words without loss of clarity, and elision characterizes both a great deal of regional speech idiom and the compression he prized in poetry. *Back out of all this* [unspecified noun] [which is] *now too much for us* [to handle]: it might take a few or a hundred readings to parse that, but we can.

Again largely because ours is not an inflected language, so-called natural or normal English syntax places the controlling subject, verb, and object at the head of the sentence before branching off into elaboration, as in lines 18–19:

**You must** not **mind** a certain **coolness** from him
Still said to haunt this side of Panther Mountain.

But there are many familiar exceptions to this fundament-first position. The branching syntax that opens "Directive" does not follow the independent clause *(There is a house)* but introduces and restricts it; this is a "periodic sentence"—the elaborate introductory material (modification) delays the subject and predicate. The brain isn't perplexed: it knows to suspend comprehension until the fundament is revealed, the eye moving from twigs and branches to the trunk of the tree.

Similar to this, but less linear, is when a modifying string of words is used as "interruptive" syntax—that is, subordinate material divides subject-verb-object one from another for suspenseful delay (lines 8–10):

The **road** there

    *—if you'll let a guide direct you / Who only has at*

        *heart your getting lost—*

**May seem** . . .

The markers "if" and "who" alert us that the upcoming chunks of language are subordinate to the deep structure, to be held in abeyance as we wait for the predicate. We can get the same signal from prepositions, like these that separate the verb from its object in lines 55–57:

**I have kept hidden**

    *—in the instep arch / Of an old cedar at the*

        *waterside—*

A broken drinking **goblet** . . .

And so adept is the brain at retrieving the English fundament from elaborate surfaces that natural order may be partially or even entirely reversed, "inverted"— an arrangement found not only in bad verse but some famously good poetry as well ("About suffering they were never wrong, the Old Masters . . ."). Inversion controls most interrogatory sentences *(Where were they all not twenty years ago?),* expletives *(There is . . .),* and dependent clauses that elide the subordinating pronoun *(Great monolithic knees* [which] *the former town / Long since gave up pretense of keeping covered . . .).* Because inversions are so familiar to us in ordinary English speech, these examples by Frost sound every bit as natural as "natural" word order.

Like the engine of a train, the fundament may appear almost anywhere in the sentence, pushing some of its boxcars and pulling others. Inverted, interruptive, introductory, periodic, elided, right-branching, parallel, hypotactic—these terms name common syntactical patterns, or surface structures, quickly recognized by the English-speaking brain, efficient delivery systems for often-complicated discursive information. They also identify a few of the tools writers in English use to manipulate pattern and variation, elements indispensable to any art.

In literature, of course, syntax does more than deliver discursive information. Each of Frost's sentences is also an expressive organization of sound, placed in pleasing or provocative relation to other sentences. Compelling syntactical rhythm, like musical phrasing in Jourdain's description, "lacks the repetitive, evenly paced accentuations of measured rhythm . . . [and] is built up by a succession of irregular sonic shapes that combine in various ways like the parts of a painting, sometimes hanging in exquisite balance, sometimes joining forces to gyrate or plunge or swirl." Essentially, composers create a syntax, using rhythmic, melodic, and harmonic markers to create phrases or chunks with which to build "complex hierarchies"—such as when, Joudain says,

> [r]iding a melodic line, harmony wanders into un-
> familiar territory then returns to momentary repose.
> Upon hearing this resolution, a brain groups the pre-
> ceding notes, then readies itself to perceive the next
> progression. Lesser resolutions create lesser phrases
> that can be built into hierarchies of larger ones.

A similar set of lesser resolutions is at work in the following passage from Maeve Brennan's short story "The Poor Men and Women":

> The priest's mother was distracted with herself, wake-
> ful, impenitent, heated in every part by a wearisome

discontent that had begun in her spirit very young. She wore herself out cleaning her house, going over her rooms with her dry violent hands, scraping and plucking and picking and rubbing the walls and floors and furniture, and stopping in the middle to clench her fingers tight, tight, tight, but not tight enough, never enough for her, there was no tightness hard and fast enough to satisfy her. Therefore she continued in want.

We can easily parse the separate grammatical units of Brennan's opening sentence: *priest's mother/*subject, *was distracted/*verb phrase, *with herself/*modifying prepositional phrase, etc. But as we sight-read, we are responding to the rhythms of the language stream, to its musical phrasing, and the compelling feature of this particular sentence sound is the self-correcting list that dominates its second half. When the predicate arrives—and there's no waiting as with Frost—we take its chunk in a single gulp: *was-distracted-with-herself.* Now that the fundament is in place, the woman's slightly odd, slightly vague condition is immediately elaborated (again, no waiting), for greater clarity, with three small red balls on the crib toy of the observation, three modifiers:

wakeful, impenitent, heated . . . ,

the last of these a syntactical echo of the initial participle *(distracted).* But any balance or closure achieved by that frame is undone by subsequent right-branching, which overbalances the little list with yet more prepositions and a subordinate clause as the sentence continues to unfurl:

> wakeful,
> impenitent,
> heated in every part by a wearisome discontent
> > that had begun in her spirit very young.

Isolated adjectives and a fat chunk: symmetrical in function, asymmetrical in rhythm.

In the next sentence, which also puts the fundament first, parallel participial chunks accomplish a similar effect:

> She wore herself out
> > **cleaning** her house,
> > **going** over her rooms with her dry violent
> > > hands . . .
> > **rubbing** the walls and floors and furniture,
> > and **stopping** in the middle . . .

There is, however, a further complication. Midway in this sequence, following those again unbalancing prepositions *(over . . . with),* Brennan doubles the parallelism with a second, interior list, a clutch of unadorned, half-rhymed participles—**scraping** and **plucking** and **picking** and **rubbing**. And that triggers yet another interior list, this time compound objects *(the walls and floors and furniture),* and then explodes in a sort of editorial outburst:

> stopping in the middle to clench her fingers tight, tight, tight, but not tight enough, never enough for her, there was no tightness hard and fast enough to satisfy her.

Like an extended musical phrase, the sentence has a shape—it branches, swells, obsesses, idles, and swells again into perseveration across the comma splice and through a new independent clause to the period.

If what is said, not how, were all that mattered, Brennan might have stopped here, with the revelation of character made dramatic and convincing by the accelerating repetition. But she scores her stories another way. The paragraph has a shape, too, the long second sentence undercut rhythmically and reinforced thematically: *Therefore she continued in want.* That final short assertion raps out judgment as unequivocally as a gavel.

This huge variation in overall sentence length, and in the length of the chunks within the sentences, creates surprise and energy. Meanwhile, all three sentences share a declarative pattern—fundament at the head, modification trailing after it. This kind of sentence is sufficiently characteristic to be called part of Brennan's prose style, but so is the musical phrasing that shapes the paragraph into an arc: crescendo with abrupt denouement. The woman's furious discontent, and the unrelieved cost of it, are not only expressed in her actions but enacted in the song of the prose. The final fundament and its prepositional phrase *(she continued in want)* duplicate the paragraph's initial syntax *(The priest's mother was distracted with herself)*, and thereby complete a frame within which the character frets and rages and cannot change. Stopping short of the earlier elaboration, its parallel and right-branching modification, this final, unadorned, simple declarative sentence clicks the passage shut like a coffin lid. It also marks the end of a "distinct musical shape," the first large chunk of Brennan's "complex hierarchies," her characteristic arrangements of pattern and variation, balance and asymmetry, repetition and surprise.

By "characteristic," we usually mean a writer's stylistic fingerprints: no one would ever confuse an unattributed paragraph by Brennan with a paragraph by, say, Hemingway or Henry James. In each case, the writer's preference for certain arrangements of syntax—the order of the words in the sentence, the order of the sentences themselves—is unmistakable. For the past one hundred years, poets have meanwhile been fretting about the poetic line, what it might be, what it can do, when released from a priori metric patterns. It is useful to remember that we write in sentences too, and that the infinite variations of generative syntax take another quantum leap when they can be reinforced, or reconfigured—rechunked—by the poetic line.

# The Sentence and the Line

Phrasing in music, says Robert Jourdain, is the rhythmic system that builds "large-scale musical objects and thereby induc[es] large-scale musical perceptions." Its arrangement is an enactment of form. But another kind of rhythm is also present in music: meter, a pattern of accentuated beats. And "[a]t the core of meter is pulse, an unceasing clock-beat that rhythmic patterns overlay."

> The two conceptions of rhythm are sometimes referred to as vocal (for phrasing) and instrumental (for meter). Phrasing is "vocal" because it naturally arises from song, and thus from speech. . . . Meter . . . derives from the way we play musical instruments. . . .
>
> Meter . . . organizes small groups of notes, and sometimes larger ones, and thereby provides a sort of grid upon which music is drawn. On the other hand, phrasing imparts a kind of narrative to music. It is the mechanism by which a composition can play out a grand drama. Broadly speaking, meter organizes musical time on the small scale while phrasing organizes it on the large scale. . . . Yet . . . [t]he two kinds of rhythm are not entirely at peace with one another.

Poetic meter is more dissimilar than similar to musical meter, but poetry likewise makes use of two often-competing rhythmic systems: the rhythm of syntax I have been discussing, which poetry shares with well-made prose, and the rhythm of the line. Like musical measure, the poetic line is inherently artificial, imposed by the poet onto the language. Like musical measure, lineation can mark—signal—the chunks on which phrasing depends, as we saw in the Frost poem. Fixed meter in a poem, of course, can reinforce those markers (make them "more available to the ear" in Gilbert Murray's formulation) or can establish a competing set of phrases. But in free verse, too, the poet continually negotiates the extent to which the two rhythmic systems will be "at peace with one another." That is, whether a line will be primarily consonant with the syntax, parsing it, or dissonant, in counterpoint; and the effects of that choice seem more significantly different between short- and long-lined poems than between metered and unmetered verse.

The longevity of English pentameter, for instance, may reflect in part one of these advantageous differences. Because a decasyllabic line is longer than most of the individual units of syntax that constitute adult sentences, it can more easily participate in large-scale musical phrasing, providing the poet opportunities to combine "bite-size chunks" for new emphasis or nuance.

In the opening line of Frost's "Directive," *Back out of all this now too much for us,* "this" functions grammatically as a demonstrative pronoun standing in for an elided referent (something like "present complicated modern life"). But "this" also appears in our lexicon and our grammar as an adjective; so its placement in the metrically enclosed string of monosyllabic words, among apparently equal stresses, seems to press the adverb that follows *(now)* into service as a noun. Elided subordinating markers hover over the passage, making us reluctant to chunk the syntax definitively as either "all THIS, [which is] now too much" or "all this NOW, [which is] too much." As a result, the unbroken musical phrase created by the line of ten monosyllabic words (no colonizing those five metrical feet!) complicates the grammar and overrides the song of the syntax. Simultaneously, the syntax complicates the rhythm of the line by making word function ambiguous and thereby increasing the number of potential stresses.

On the other hand, a short line of seven or fewer syllables will usually correspond only to the smaller grammatical units, or chunks, of our surface sentence structures, and so large-scale phrasing must be left to the whole sentence, paced and punctuated by the lines (which may explain the ubiquitous reference to line "breaks" in free verse poems, rather than to the integral unit the line creates). The shorter line achieves new emphasis or nuance by increasing the frequency of temporarily suspended comprehension, separating the constituent parts of the sentence and delaying its completion, for which the brain is avid.

We can see these differences most easily by comparing two free verse poems of richly patterned syntax that is highly consonant—at peace—with lineation. My short-lined example is by Stanley Kunitz:

### King of the River

If the water were clear enough,
if the water were still,
but the water is not clear,
the water is not still,
you would see yourself,
slipped out of your skin,
nosing upstream,
slapping, thrashing,
tumbling
over the rocks
till you paint them
with your belly's blood:
Finned Ego,
yard of muscle that coils,
uncoils.

If the knowledge were given you,
but it is not given,
for the membrane is clouded
with self-deceptions
and the iridescent image swims
through a mirror that flows,
you would surprise yourself
in that other flesh
heavy with milt,
bruised, battering toward the dam
that lips the orgiastic pool.

*Come. Bathe in these waters.*
*Increase and die.*

If the power were granted you
to break out of your cells,
but the imagination fails
and the doors of the senses close
on the child within,
you would dare to be changed,
as you are changing now,
into the shape you dread
beyond the merely human.
A dry fire eats you.
Fat drips from your bones.

The flutes of your gills discolor.
You have become a ship for parasites.
The great clock of your life
is slowing down,
and the small clocks run wild.
For this you were born.
You have cried to the wind
and heard the wind's reply:
"I did not choose the way,
the way chose me."
You have tasted the fire on your tongue
till it is swollen black
with a prophetic joy:
"Burn with me!
The only music is time,
the only dance is love."

If the heart were pure enough,
but it is not pure,
you would admit
that nothing compels you
any more, nothing
at all abides,
but nostalgia and desire,
the two-way ladder
between heaven and hell.

On the threshold
of the last mystery,
at the brute absolute hour,
you have looked into the eyes
of your creature self,
which are glazed with madness,
and you say
he is not broken but endures,
limber and firm
in the state of his shining,
forever inheriting his salt kingdom,
from which he is banished
forever.

Kunitz has said, "The very first lines came to me with their conditional syntax and suspended clauses, a winding and falling movement. The rest seemed to flow." That paradigm established a high degree of consonance between line and syntax; of the poem's seventy-seven lines, only one is not end-stopped by punctuation (forty-eight of these) or what might be called end-paused (twenty-eight), unpunctuated but coincident with the syntactical chunks. At the same time, Kunitz avoids the flatness and choppiness that threaten very short lines by using energetic, densely patterned syntax throughout. Behind the first sentence is right-branching, hypotactic logic:

> If the water were clear (and still) enough,
> [then] you would see yourself nosing, slapping,
>      thrashing, tumbling,
> [you who are] Finned Ego, a yard of muscle,
> but the water is not clear and still.

Of course, Kunitz has little interest in discursive logic, and by using the line to reinforce the markers of almost every discrete syntactical unit, he can slow us up, not let us gulp the whole thing down, and rearrange the actual syntax into provocative parallelism without losing clarity. The coordinate clauses that dispel imagining *(but the water is not . . .)* appear not last but early. In this way, Kunitz admits improbability (after all, we are asked to see ourselves as fish) and quickly trumps it by returning to the subjunctive verb, made more powerful now by its position in the fundament of the sentence, more assertive: *you would see,* not just wish but equivalent claim. Moving up the coordinate clauses also allows four lines of relentless repetition—*the water, the water, the water, the water*—which fosters a formal alignment between, and a disregard for, the conjunctions, those "buts" and "ifs." Ordinarily, a coordinated (independent) "but" clause is worth more to a sentence than a restrictive (subordinate) "if" clause; Kunitz's exactly parallel lines, using a limited and reshuffled lexicon, redress the grammatical power of the rational objection.

Four of the poem's five stanzas open on this same realignment of clauses, in lines that are syntactically and metrically identical:

| | |
|---|---|
| If the water were clear enough | (stanza 1) |
| If the knowledge were given you | (stanza 2) |
| If the power were granted you | (stanza 4) |
| If the heart were pure enough | (stanza 5) |

This unvarying position in the sentence and the stanza gives the refrain a structural importance. And there's more: transitive or intransive verbs and endline repetition in these first lines yoke stanzas 1 and 5, stanzas 2 and 4. But while that is happening, the functional chunks of syntax—the introductory clauses those lines belong to—suggest an alternating, not interlocking, pattern:

2 lines of "if" in stanza 1
1 line of "if" in stanza 2
2 lines of "if" in stanza 4
1 line of "if" in stanza 5

Other parallel chunks—the "but" clauses—provide a third and unpredictable counterpoint, in which the voiced objections grow more and then less insistent:

2 lines of "but" in stanza 1
5 lines of "but" in stanza 2
3 lines of "but" in stanza 4
1 line of "but" in stanza 5

This last is pattern by syntactical function but variation in the music, in the length of those clauses. We register both the pattern and the variation because these "but" clauses are sandwiched, in each sentence, between two steady, anaphoric refrains: the opening of each stanza *(If, if, if, if),* and the fundaments with their subjunctive verbs:

| | |
|---|---|
| you would see yourself | (stanza 1) |
| you would surprise yourself | (stanza 2) |
| you would dare to be changed | (stanza 4) |
| you would admit | (stanza 5) |

I suspect we could not absorb all this, even subliminally, and also follow the plot line, in a prose paragraph or in highly enjambed, dissonant lineation. Here, the short consonant lines release well-marked grammatical units to us one at a time, helping us parse the complicated surface structure and register its recurrences. Meanwhile, uneven stanza and sentence length bring energy and variation into the poem, forming the larger chunks with which Kunitz builds "large-scale musical objects" and enacts form:

Stanza 1: 15 lines, 1 sentence
Stanza 2: 11 lines, 1 sentence
Stanza 3: 2 lines, 3 sentences
Stanza 4: 27 lines, 10 sentences (one of 9 lines,
    5 of 1 line each)
Stanza 5: 22 lines, 2 sentences (9 lines and 13 lines)

Exactly as Jourdain describes musical phrasing: "a succession of irregular sonic shapes that combine in various ways like the parts of a painting." Those shapes are clearly marked for us; even though stanza lengths are unpredictable, each stanza is closed, end-stopped, completed in the syntax. And after each of these lesser resolutions, we return to the familiar starting place; the brain "groups the preceding notes, then readies itself to perceive the next progression."

Tethered so firmly in the poem's overall structure, stanza 4 can substantially vary its musical phrasing for energy and surprise without threatening coherence. There, the long hypotactic sentences yield to a flurry of short ones, increasing the occasions for full end stops with those paratactic declaratives, which are reinforced, never subdivided, by the lineation:

A dry fire eats you.
Fat drips from your bones.
The flutes of your gills discolor.
You have become a ship for parasites.

We should also note that this stanza, the longest in the poem, has no caesuras (midline punctuation). The other four stanzas have only one each, the last of them, at line 60, enabling the poem's only true enjambment:

> any more, nothing
> at all abides . . .

That is, no more than five times out of seventy-seven do the rhythmic phrases of the line or the syntax in any way syncopate or subdivide or override one another. Instead, throughout the poem, there is persistent formal fidelity to the small syntactical chunks. The result, even without a fixed line length, is that the line provides a dependable unit of measure—a pace if not a pulse—and this organizes musical time on the small scale. Meanwhile, sentence structure and stanza organize musical time on the large scale, combining the small chunks into larger chunks, the lesser resolutions and phrases into complex hierarchies. Thus Kunitz orchestrates the two rhythmic systems. The tempo is *adagio,* the tone *mysterioso*—effects achieved not with lineation alone but the interplay of line and syntax.

The relationship between the two is just as vigorous in "Song of a Man Who Has Come Through," by D. H. Lawrence (whom Kunitz has admired). But here, although equally consonant with the syntax, the line participates actively in the large-scale phrasing of a poem every bit as ecstatic as Kunitz's:

> Not I, not I, but the wind that blows through me!
> A fine wind is blowing the new direction of Time.
> If only I let it bear me, carry me, if only it carry me!
> If only I am sensitive, subtle, oh, delicate, a winged gift!
> If only, most lovely of all, I yield myself and am
>     borrowed
> By the fine, fine wind that takes its course through
>     the chaos of the world
> Like a fine, an exquisite chisel, a wedge-blade inserted;
> If only I am keen and hard like the sheer tip of a wedge
> Driven by invisible blows,
> The rock will split, we shall come at the wonder, we
>     shall find the Hesperides.
>
> Oh, for the wonder that bubbles into my soul,
> I would be a good fountain, a good well-head,
> Would blur no whisper, spoil no expression.
>
> What is the knocking?
> What is the knocking at the door in the night?
> It is somebody wants to do us harm.
>
> No, no, it is the three strange angels.
> Admit them, admit them.

Kunitz has only one true enjambment in seventy-seven short lines, Lawrence has none at all in his eighteen substantially longer lines, and yet the pace of the two poems could hardly differ more. The two rhythmic systems have largely traded duties. Kunitz's first stanza, in fifteen lines and a single sentence, encompassed 55 words; Lawrence's, in three sentences and only ten lines, has 115 words. Combining—chunking together—the discrete grammatical units Kunitz kept apart, lines here are not the micromanagers, the pulse, the grid for the musical phrasing of the syntax; they are macromanagers, the very source of musical phrasing, and the poet wields these long lines with gusto, hurling large chunks at us, creating a "torrent" of words he wants us to gulp down whole, or be battered by. Frost complained that free verse was like playing tennis "with the net down," but Lawrence redefines the game as racquetball, each line another hard shot, direct or crosscourt, forehand or backhand, against the end-stop wall.

The first two lines provide a sort of prologue to the poem and introduce a persistent adjective and noun *(fine wind)*. An initial direct repetition (two strokes—*Not I, not I*) and a heavy end stop (!) frame and contain line 1, a statement missing its verb. Line 2 is roughly the same length, also end-stopped but gently, a simple declarative in natural order, undivided by punctuation; by according us the poem's first clear fundament *(wind is blowing)*, it fulfills or completes line 1.

But following that syntactic couplet, we must hang on for a periodic sentence of repeating, anaphoric, asymmetrical, unpredictable introductory clauses—the rest of the stanza. Kunitz's "if" clauses were large-scale patterns, a structural refrain that marked and linked the stanzas' irregular sonic shapes. Here, the line itself creates irregular sonic shapes as it compels the overlapping syntactical chunks "to gyrate or plunge or swirl":

If only I let it bear me, carry me, if only it carry me!

As in that third sentence in Maeve Brennan's "The Poor Men and Women," the second half of line 3 is doing rhythmic but not discursive work, which is also true of line 4:

If only I am sensitive, subtle, oh, delicate, a winged gift!

Four synonymous modifiers, interrupted by an intensifier: cast in the short, consonant lineation Kunitz uses, this degree of reiteration would drag the poem into torpor. Instead, the long, propulsive musical phrasing drives the list straight into the exclamatory wall.

Then Lawrence starts over at the same spot *(If only),* piling up interruptive syntax, compound action, right-branching, and repetition in a great *appassionato* crescendo:

> If only, most lovely of all, I yield myself and am
>     borrowed
> By the fine, fine wind that takes its course through
>     the chaos of the world . . .

which is then gradually slowed, double-stitched, and end-stopped:

> Like a fine, an exquisite chisel, a wedge-blade
>     inserted; . . .

In line 7, caesuras, like Kunitz's short lines, step us through three distinct rhythmic units, each a single beat longer than the one preceding: *like a fine,     an exquisite chisel,     a wedge-blade inserted.* The comparison is actually a single figure made of paired adjectives, paired nouns: *fine/exquisite, chisel/wedge-blade.* But the commas have regrouped its parts, parceling out one per chunk. With the long conjoining line, Lawrence can have it both ways: pairs in the syntactical logic and a triad in the rhythm for resolution.

A "lesser resolution," that is, because the sentence is not yet complete. And so it backs up again to the anaphora *(if only),* another pair of modifiers *(keen and hard),* another simile using the same object *(wedge),* another set of now-branching descriptors *(like the tip     of a wedge* [that is] *driven     by blows)*—it is leaping from the backs of the previous lines, one might say, for the last great push, through and past the first unpunctuated line since line 2:

> If only I am keen and hard like the sheer tip of a wedge
> Driven by invisible blows, . . .

End stop, deep breath, brief rest, before Lawrence delivers, at last, the fundament—the three asymmetrical chunks of the long-delayed, parallel, paratactic independent clauses:

> The rock will split, we shall come at the wonder, we
>      shall find the Hesperides.

A periodic sentence without peer, as two counterpointed patterns grapple within the syntax. The doubling inside the lines is fairly obvious:

> Not I, not I . . .
> If only . . . if only, carry me . . . carry me!
> fine, fine . . .
> we shall, we shall . . .

Less obvious, perhaps, but crucial to the momentum, is the repetition from line to line—anaphora *(If only)* but also *wind* (lines 1, 2, 6), *fine* (wind and chisel), *wedge-blade* and *wedge,* in a pairing action that is completed—resolved—overturned—by the triad of the fundament (line 10), which returns, triumphant, to the triple phrasing of lines 1, 3, and 7. For all its heedless ecstasy, this is a wonderfully controlled, extremely shapely sentence and stanza.

That same counterpoint, three against two, finds surprising uses in the rest of the poem. As if to bring us up slowly from the swift crosscurrents of stanza 1, Lawrence puts next a stanza of three end-stopped lines, a single sentence built on, and lineated for, absolute doubling of syntax and lexicon:

> would be . . . would blur
> good fountain, good well-head
> no whisper . . . no expression.

Unlike Kunitz's sudden terse couplet, this stanza is no pivot, swinging us back into sweep and extension. Instead, Lawrence moves to another threesome of end-stopped lines, this time each line its own sentence, the first of them forming the poem's second four-word line—

> What is the knocking?

the second an extension of it—

What is the knocking at the door in the night?

If his stanzas were as consonant with syntax as Kunitz's had been, these two questions would be honored formally as a couplet. But Lawrence again asserts the triad, providing an answer to the repeated question:

What is the knocking?
What is the knocking at the door in the night?
It is somebody wants to do us harm.

As a result, the funneling down from his long, headlong first stanza stalls in an extraordinarily quiet moment here, a space before closure. The tercet has meanwhile divided another matched pair of end-stopped sentences, the false answer countered and corrected:

It is somebody wants to do us harm.

No, no, it is the three strange angels.

Syntactical pattern makes sure we hear the pairings—two questions, two answers. Formal arrangement (line and stanza) regroups them with a coda: a final couplet, to match the opening:

No, no, it is the three strange angels.
Admit them, admit them.

This last pairing combines correction and action, introduces a new kind of sentence (imperative), and echoes the initial insistent doubling *(Not I, not I)* for quiet but powerful final resolution.

Kunitz has said, "You cannot write a poem until you hit upon its rhythm. That rhythm not only belongs to the subject matter, it belongs to your interior world, and the moment they hook up there's a quantum leap of energy. You can ride on that rhythm, it will carry you somewhere strange." That rhythm in "King of the River," he has made clear, sprang from two braided sources, with even the opening lines authoritative in "their conditional syntax and suspended clauses, a winding and falling movement." In the Lawrence poem as well, the rhythm of the poem depends utterly on the same two sources. Whether line and syntax are consonant with one another, as they are in these poems, or set in muscular opposition, as they are in poems I will examine next, it is the dynamic interplay between them that comprises the prosody of almost all memorable poetry in English, in forms both fixed and "free."

# Meter and Phrase

Vocal rhythm (phrasing), which organizes musical time on the large scale, and instrumental rhythm (meter), which organizes it on the small scale: the distinction Jourdain points out in music is essentially the same one Frost made for poetry. "A sentence," he said, "is not interesting merely in conveying a meaning of words. It must do something more: it must convey a meaning by sound."

Long before there were any confirming MRI scans, he called these "sentence sounds" "the sound of sense," out of which "I . . . consciously set myself to make music." In his formulation, "dramatic tones of meaning" come from phrasing, from "vital sentences" (as opposed to merely "grammatical sentences") apprehended by the ear. These are "struck across a limited meter" to create "endless possibilities for tune."

> [I]t's a tune of the blend of those two things [sense and meter]. Something rises—it's neither one of these things. It's neither the meter nor the rhythm; it's a tune arising from the stress on those, same as your fingers on the strings, you know. The twang!

Two elements, as Jourdain has said about music, "not entirely at peace with one another," and as early as 1913–14, Frost claimed in letters from England that he was "never more pleased than when I can get these into strained relation," insisting on the importance of the vernacular, the poet's need to "catch [sentence sounds] fresh from talk," to "learn to get cadences by skillfully breaking the sounds of sense with all their irregularity of accent across the regular beat of the metre." But his formulation of this tension in 1951, in a different historical context, can be seen as containing a different emphasis: "Poetry plays the rhythms of dramatic speech on the grid of meter."

For Frost, that fixed grid was crucial: "All I ask is iambic. . . . The crossed swords are always the same. The sword dancer varies his position between them." Despite the confident rhetoric, the crossed swords are not *always* the same—not even in his own poems: a reader would weary of either relentless iambic or insistent "twang!" What the figure shows is the temperament behind Frost's famous put-down: that free verse is like tennis with the net down. Less well known is Charles Wright's parry: that free verse is actually the high-wire act without the net. Frost worried he would "be lost in the air with just cutting loose"—cutting loose, that is, from iambic measure "as rigid as two crossed swords in the Sword Dance." But the high-wire walker, far from "cutting loose," depends absolutely, thrillingly, on the thin line along which he inches his slippered feet.

Wright's metaphor corrects Frost's assertion that in unmetered poems something essential is missing. Rather, it reminds us, the issues of pattern and variation, tension and release, shape and energy—matters of form, that is—remain the same, to be negotiated poet by poet, poem by poem, line by line, in verse both fixed and "free." A priori parameters are never more than a partial (and in some hands superficial) solution. Frost himself insisted that "the living part of a poem is the intonation entangled somehow in the syntax idiom and meaning of a sentence." We saw this enacted by Kunitz and Lawrence, who found an alternative for "the other thing—something . . . for me to put a strain on." Instead of Frost's rigid crossed swords, both Kunitz's "King of the River" and Lawrence's "The Man Who Has Come Through" use a faithful coincidence between the syntax and the line for that productive discipline.

In the Lawrence poem, the long line, making its own "sound of sense," combines—chunks together—small grammatical units that are often appositive and even synonymous, and then with end pause or end stop divides that musical phrase from the even longer sentence. Because the line lengths vary widely, pattern must derive from syntax, through similarities in sentence structure, and from lexical repetition, both of which are absorbed or emphasized by the line's chunking, end stop, and anaphora. As with Whitman (an obvious progenitor), Lawrence gives formal authority to the large-scale forward momentum of the "sentence sound," and thus emphasizes with the line what Jourdain calls the "narrative" of the composition, its "grand drama"—effects removed if we recast the poem into Kunitz's short line:

> If only I let it bear me, carry me,
> if only it carry me!
> If only I am sensitive, subtle,
> oh, delicate,
> a winged gift!
> If only, most lovely of all,
> I yield myself
> and am borrowed
> by the fine, fine wind
> that takes its course
> through the chaos
> of the world . . .

Isolated this way, the repetitions become tedious and self-indulgent, the text static and overwritten, burdened by a nonfunctional form.

Conversely, a long, inclusive line would be completely inappropriate for Kunitz's series of assertions, sometimes thorny, sometimes breezy, his moments of sly reversal and qualification. Chunking the logical parentheticals alongside his conditionals—

If the heart were pure enough, but it is not pure . . .

—would produce self-canceling units of thought, undermining the authority of the voice. And larger line chunks would also send the concrete narrative and imagistic parts of the poem flying too quickly past:

nosing upstream, slapping, thrashing, tumbling over
    the rocks
till you paint them with your belly's blood: . . .

In other words, a *short* parsing line is crucial to the Kunitz poem where, as Frost recommends, large-scale musical phrasing is managed not by the line but by syntax—in this case, complex syntax reiterative not chunk by chunk but in its recursive patterns, sentence by sentence, stanza by stanza. While Lawrence's lines drive us past syntactic markers and combine distinct grammatical units into sweeping, propulsive musical phrases, Kunitz uses end-paused and end-stopped lineation to separate those units. This provides stability and clarity, parceling out the composite pieces of his long hypotactic sentences or exaggerating the directness of his short declaratives in stanzas 3 and 4. The choice slows us down, bringing to the poem a stateliness of tone, a studied persuasion, not possible with Lawrence's rushing tempo. Marked—doubly paused—by the parsing lineation, the composite pieces of Kunitz's sentences take on a rough rhythmic equivalence, the hierarchy of grammar now democratized by form. Meanwhile, that particular formal arrangement contains enough rudimentary pattern, in the syntactical integrity of the lines, to suggest "a sort of grid upon which the music is played."

Kunitz's may seem especially subtle and elastic, but the grid in memorable English language poetry, even in metered verse—even in Frost's own "strictly" iambic verse—can never do more than approximate the practical math of musical meter, which controls duration utterly. A quarter note sounds in the air exactly one fourth as long as a whole note, half as long as a half note, twice as long as an eighth note; exceptions must be clearly and deliberately notated (triplets, for instance, or a *fermata*). This is what provides a steady pulse, despite the pitch or dynamic level of the notes, within the chosen tempo, and that pulse can be altered significantly only with an all-alert inserted on the score *(rubato, rallentando, accelerando)*. Fixed equivalence of the parts is what allowed polyphony: instruments, or singers, or both, can pursue separate yet simultaneous musical phrases and predictably coincide with one another as intended. (A performer's annotation of such rigid equivalence—delaying, anticipating, flirting with the beat while the beat goes on—is the primary stuff of jazz.) Musical meter in collaboration with language can easily override inherent linguistic pauses and stresses however it wishes, insisting that the words march to its tyrannical drum. Gounod's popular "Ave Maria," for instance, contains the following rescoring of lexical proportion: AAAH (6 beats) – Ve (1½ beats) Ma – (½ beat) REE (4 beats) – AH (4 beats).

By contrast, metric in English poetry combines individual sounds already and intractably various in duration, precisely because they are not mechanically produced (instrumental) but are vocal, both formed in the mouth and necessarily faithful to the rhythms of the language. Our phrases "never mind" and "my oh my" are each three syllables long, but while the three long vowels of the second phrase make its three syllables approximate, the same cannot be said of the first three. Nor are the two phrases equivalent in any musically meaningful way. Syllabic measure, then, in English, may indicate the number of pieces of fruit in the bowl but fails to distinguish grapes from bananas. Whatever its uses to the poet or the reader, it is abstract rather than pragmatic, and thus a long way from musical meter.

Accentual measure at least relies on a pattern the ear can discern. Again, however, in English poetry we measure accents by simply counting them, ignoring subtle differences in duration and pitch. Our polyglot language comprises syllables of hugely varying weight and worth, blending polysyllabic Latinate words and Teutonic monosyllables, irregular verbs and Greek prefixes, pace-slowing clusters of consonants or resonant long vowels. Poetry that aims to make meaning must balance the recurring and intoxicating patterns of song against the familiar patterns in the language. Any versification that wishes to be strictly mathematical may run aground on the shoals of a poem's most essential material.

Ever conscripting, adapting, recycling, and redefining words, English depends heavily on lexical stress to indicate their denotations; stresses fix in place the *relative* duration of the syllables. When two words look the same (**con**-tent vs. con-**tent**, **pro**-test vs. pro-**test**, **min**-ute vs. mi-**nute**), the position of the stress can indicate differing grammatical functions, such as noun, verb, or adjective. In inflected languages, the ending of a noun will indicate its usage (subject, direct or indirect object), and therefore can appear confidently in any number of places in the sentence. In English, some pronouns retain traces of this *(I, me, my, mine)*, but primarily the objective and dative cases must be suggested either by syntactical order ("The groom gave the bride the ring" vs. "Her father gave the bride away") or by explicit function words ("We gave our gift *to* the bride"). Likewise, inflected verbs contain the subject pronoun: *veni, vidi, vici;* in English, any trace inflection ("I give, he gives") may disappear in some verb tenses "gave" or "will give"), requiring stated pronouns or a context that suggests them. Function words—including articles and even the copulative verbs "is" or "seems" or "feels"—are recognized by the brain and then forgotten: only what is semantically significant stands out— is stressed—for quick parsing. To a listener of English, "SomeONE gave THE bride THE ring" sounds like the speech of another species.

Sometimes, of course, poets *mean* to rescore syntax, and rhetoric is a third source of linguistic stress, a common means of clarity, precision, and tone in everyday speech. Frank Bidart is our current genius of rhetorical stress in poetry:

> The reason I *know* I am *NOT* insane
> Is because, unlike my brother,
>
> I *feel guilt.*

But rescoring does not always require typographical aids. Sometimes context or syntactical structure will do the job, emphasizing, in the following, the modifiers, the numerical pronouns, or the nouns:

> That ring is mine, not this one.
> I gave her not that one but these two.
> The ring is mine, the dress is mine, and the veil is also
>    mine.

And sometimes poets will impose rhetorical emphasis by way of musical stress derivative of pattern:

> There is a house that is no more a house
> Upon a farm that is no more a farm
> And in a town that is no more a town.

In summary, the rhythms embedded in the language include not only the large-scale phrasing of syntax but small-scale arrangements as well, relationships among stressed and unstressed syllables that can support or resist poetic meter. Accentual-syllabic meter may have achieved its hegemony in English by accommodating just such arrangements: it seeks to organize what is already inherent and essential. In this prosody, pattern is not only quantitative, like syllabic and accentual verse, but qualitative as well, attending to the placement of a stress relative to unstressed syllables that surround it. One counts not just syllables or stresses but units ("feet"), of two or three syllables each, in which the ratio can be observed and can recur. That ratio is heard to have one of two essential characteristics: either rising toward the stress (*iambic, - /,* or *anapestic, - - /*), or else falling away from it (*trochaic, / -,* or *dactylic, / - -*). "Duple" or "triple" meter indicates how many syllables usually occur within the unit, and Greek prefixes *(di-, tri-, tetra-, penta-, hexa-)* quantify the stress-defined units in the line.

It is possible, of course, that verse can adhere with technological fervor to these patterns, even reinforce them with rhyme and other emphatic devices, and remain recognizable as English speech: some nursery rhymes do just that. But the rhythm of a memorable poem is muscular, not merely skeletal: to say such a poem is "iambic" is only to name the predominant pattern. Exceptions—variants—are easily available from the language itself. Poets frequently substitute a spondaic foot, uniting two consecutive stresses *(blackboard, pushpin, lockjaw, tailspin);* use a reversed foot, to counter and syncopate the line's rising or falling impulse; or at line's end either add an unstressed syllable to the rising rhythm (feminine ending) or drop one from the last trochaic foot. Meanwhile, other more subtle variations are caused by long vowels or plosive consonants, which effect duration but don't always show up in a metric scansion.

As a result, unlike the largely quantitative poetics of French or the accentual verse of Anglo-Saxon, most of the great metered poetry in English offers, in its accentual syllabics, only a very flexible grid indeed, a sort of palimpsest behind the pauses, stresses, chunking, and syntactical rhythms of speech. The following paradigmatic sonnet (Shakespeare's 29) should demonstrate:

> When, in disgrace with fortune and men's eyes,
> I all alone beweep my outcast state,
> And trouble deaf heaven with my bootless cries,
> And look upon myself, and curse my fate,
> Wishing me like to one more rich in hope,
> Featured like him, like him with friends possess'd,
> Desiring this man's art and that man's scope,
> With what I most enjoy contented least;
> Yet in these thoughts myself almost despising
> Haply I think on thee—and then my state,
> Like to the lark at break of day arising
> From sullen earth, sings hymns at heaven's gate;
> For thy sweet love remember'd such wealth brings
> That then I scorn to change my state with kings.

An untortured reading of the first four lines sounds something like this:

> **When**, in dis-**grace** with **for**-tune and **men's eyes**,
> I **all** a-**lone** be-**weep** my **out-cast state**,

And **troub**-le **deaf heav'**n with my **boot**-less **cries**,
And **look** upon my**self**, and **curse** my **fate**, . . .

We routinely refer to this poem's rhythm as iambic
pentameter, implying five stressed and five unstressed
syllables in every line; but while the iambic foot is the
most prominent in this quatrain, no line of it consists
only of iambs. One can of course assign variant feet in
order to count five small units in each decasyllabic line,
but the accentual part is more slippery. Line 2 seems
to have six speech stresses, while line 4 may have only
four—lexically, *upon* carries more emphasis on the second syllable than on the first, but prepositions, merely
function words, are essentially unheard unless stressed
rhetorically or metrically, and we haven't had enough
clear pentameter to command the metrical stress.

Although the poem thus far hints at meter, what
dominates is not an insistent, instrumental pulse but the
vocal phrasing determined by the syntax. That syntax
opens on a subordinate clause with introductory modifiers (line 1) and four compound verb phrases: the first
two of these phrases, roughly the same in length, appear
unbroken in the end-stopped lines 2 and 3; the last two,
shorter, are chunked together in line 4. What the brain
"hears" as it works rapidly to decode the language is not
four equivalent line chunks but a sequence of unequal

rhythmic units that swell and then diminish, drawn by transitive verbs:

> When,
> in disgrace with fortune and men's eyes,
> I all alone beweep my outcast state,
> And trouble deaf heaven with my bootless cries,
> And look upon myself,
> and curse my fate, . . .

At quatrain's end, although the second hard rhyme signals resolution, the brain knows otherwise: the poem's initial conjunction *(When)* had "marked" all of it as subordinate. We keep reading to find the fundamental subject and predicate of this hypotactic sentence—which are further delayed in the next four lines also, by syntax even less grammatically significant, phrases made from parallel present participles—

> **Wishing** me like to one more rich in hope,
> **Desiring** this man's art and that man's scope, . . .

And each of these in turn is modified by past participles that lead, right-branching, to yet another subordinate clause nestled inside the first one:

**Featured** like him,
**Possessed** like him with friends,
**Contented** least with *what I most enjoy . . .*

We become aware of a grid for this music only gradually. After lines 5 and 6 begin with falling rhythm *(Wish-ing me . . . , Fea-tured like . . .)*, the stanza settles into initial iambs *(De-sir-ing this . . . , With what I most . . .)*. But this second quatrain also packs the lines with additional stresses—and uses balanced syntax and repetition to do so, adding rhetorical stress to monosyllabic words:

**Wish**-ing me **like** to **one more rich** in **hope**,
**Fea**-tured like **him**, **like him** with **friends** po-**ssess'd**,
De-**sir**-ing **this man's art** and **that man's scope**, . . .

In the chunking of line 6, parallel syntax *(featured . . . possessed . . .)* is rearranged after the caesura to create close repetition *(like him, like him).* This complicates the smooth iambs easily available ("featured like him, possessed like him with friends"), even as the stanza's final modifying syntax is inverted in order to achieve them. Finally, Shakespeare closes the eight-line-long introductory clause (and the strikingly Petrarchan octave) on the poem's first exactly iambic pentameter line, one that is completely consistent with lexical, syntactical, and rhetorical stresses:

> With **what** I **most** en-**joy** con-**tent**-ed **least**; . . .

The two stanzas are yoked in a formal architecture: line 8 resolves the asymmetry and suspension that precede it.

Syntax, however, is not resolved—we are still waiting for the fundament—and Shakespeare is not finished with his variations. What opens the third quatrain is one more syntactic delay, one more metrical substitution and an extra syllable:

> **Yet** in these **thoughts** my-**self** al-**most** [alt., **al**-most]
> de-**spis**-ing . . .

The feminine ending here, the poem's first, helps tumble us into the initial stress of another reversed foot in the next line before alliteration pounds the iambs like stakes into the ground:

> **Hap**-ly I **think** on **thee**—and **then** my **state**, . . .

This is precisely the moment when the poet finally delivers his first independent clause *(I think)*, the long-awaited fundament of the periodic sentence. From this point on, the formal music—the varied, muscular iambic pentameter—arm-wrestles the syntax for control, and that tension will set up the most ecstatic and musically interesting place in the poem. After the double conjunction *(and then),* which alerts us to an upcoming compound, the second subject-noun *(state)* is left hanging at the end of the line, divided from its predicate by a comma and this chunk of interruptive modification:

**Like** to the **lark** at **break** of **day** a-**ris**-ing . . .

As in the previous line, Shakespeare uses small-scale music to reinforce the iambic thrust rising out of the initial substitution, the two unstressed syllables (both insignificant function words) seeking the stress. A dense collaboration of alliteration *(Like-Lark),* half rhyme *(liKe-larK-breaK),* and long vowels (I-AH-AY-AY-I) gathers momentum, spills past the decasyllabic limit and the rhyme *(despising/arising),* and this time is not contained by punctuated end stop. Instead, the right-branching syntax pours down through the series of prepositions *(to . . . at . . . of)* and the naturally rising rhythm of their grammatical phrases. This highlights each monosyllabic noun *(lark . . . break . . . day)* and makes an irresistible extension past the line end:

**Like** to the **lark** at **break** of **day** a-**ris**-ing / from **sull**-en **earth**. . . .

The contract with the reader—that each line will be coincident to, consonant with, syntactical rhythm—has been broken, just as the simile provides the last delay, holding the reader off from the second predicate in the compound, a verb for "my state." Everything in the poem—the consistent end stops, the emerging meter, the thickening texture of vowels and consonants, the sudden enjambment, and most particularly the long periodic sentence with its parallel and then interruptive modification—has conspired to deliver the strongest possible double stress on that second predicate and its object:

> **Like** to the **lark** at **break** of **day** a-**ris**-ing
> from **sull**-en **earth**, **SINGS HYMNS** at **heav**-en's **gate**;

We can feel the formal resolution there in line 12, supplied by rhyme, a return to end stop, and a now audible pattern of iambic pentameter invigorated with one of Shakespeare's characteristic variations (spondaic substitution). This reinforces the sense of resolution, the satisfaction we feel when the sentence seems to end here, a completed thought at argument's end and fortune's reversal.

The couplet, then, with its multiple subordinate clauses, its matched unbroken decasyllabics, and its *aa* close rhymes chiming with that last verb *(sings-brings-kings),* serves as a kind of envoi:

> For **thy sweet love** re-**mem**-ber'd **such wealth
>     brings**
> That **then** I **scorn** to **change** my **state** with **kings**.

The metric in line 13 is characteristically Shakespearean. Securing the line around the poem's last polysyllabic word *(re-**mem**-ber'd),* there are two spondees, the first slowed by long vowels *(thy sweet love),* the second by mouth-gumming consonants jammed together in inverted verb and object *(such wealth brings).* But variations yield again to pattern, tension to final resolution. Exclusively monosyllabic, line 14 combines perfectly exact iambic pentameter and perfectly idiomatic phrasing; the stresses land naturally on the key words of the clause, and the negligible function words *(that ... I ... to ... my ... with)* fall to the side, leaving an ideal précis: ***then    scorn    change    state    kings***. Only here do we find the rhythms of speech and meter entirely "at peace with one another," the regular instrumental pattern coincident with the vocal phrasing; it orchestrates the unmistakable and gratifying closure. And a précis of the whole—a syntactical structure, *When ... then*—is firmly embedded in a formal arrangement compatible with the sounds of English speech, ready for Milton and Keats and hundreds of others.

# On the Grid

As a skilled dramatist, Shakespeare was a master of what Frost calls "sentence sound." In Sonnet 29 it dominates meter and rolls past the line exactly where the speaker *Haply* thinks *on thee* and is swept into joy—the climactic moment in both the dramatic situation of this lyric and the "grand drama" of its composition. Meanwhile, small-scale pattern, in the metered line, is made overt exactly where he needs its formal power to reinforce lesser or large resolutions.

Frost also said this about the sound of sense, the "dramatic tones of meaning":

> The surest way to reach the heart [of the reader] is through the ear. The visual images thrown up by a poem are important, but it is more important still to choose and arrange words in a sequence so as virtually to control the intonations and pauses of the reader's voice. By arrangement and choice of words on the part of the poet, the effects of humor, pathos, hysteria, anger, and in fact, all effects, can be indicated or obtained.

Sonnet 29 showed how this could be achieved when the poet puts syntax in charge and keeps the instrumental music muted behind it. But some of Frost's effects can also be obtained when the line consistently dominates or resists the vocal rhythms, as in the next two short metered poems I will discuss. In both of them it is not the underlying meter that is disguised or overridden—the layers in Shakespeare's palimpsest are reversed: placed front and center, the accentual-syllabic patterns seem the primary surface, with the more variable speech sounds sometimes barely discernible beneath it. The result can be another level of tone and commentary, something like a Halloween costume that outlines the human skeleton in white on the black cloth, a reminder less of death than of the person who pretends to be dead.

Perhaps "palimpsest," which implies sequence, one layer preceding the other in the time line of composition, was an inexact figure for Shakespeare's poem of angst and love, its relationship between speech and meter. In the opening quatrain, without an existing expectation of iambic pentameter, would we see it bleeding through the utterance? Certainly it is hard to imagine him relying on and then erasing more metrical regularity than what he gives us—especially after twenty-eight other sonnets and so many iambic pentameter lines in his plays. Since with every sentence we speak or read or write or listen to, the brain can easily coordinate separate modules for lexicon and syntax, the words and the arrangement of the words, surely a poet's brain, as unself-consciously as a composer's, can braid pulse and phrasing, meter and speech. As Kunitz has said, "You can ride on that rhythm, it takes you somewhere strange." Like playing the organ, or playing basketball: simultaneous hands and feet, each at their own task.

And sometimes the poet will want us to look at his feet. In Sonnet 29, we saw the powerful result when Shakespeare's delayed, complicated, varying pentameter wrested dominance away from the controlling "sentence sounds" (a single sentence at that) by conscripting syntactical minichunks to reinforce closure with perfect metrical regularity. In "The Trees," Philip Larkin uses the opposite strategy, beginning in a clear, regular pattern that will be destabilized.

> The trees are coming into leaf
> Like something almost being said;
> The recent buds relax and spread,
> Their greenness is a kind of grief.
>
> Is it that they are born again
> And we grow old? No, they die too.
> Their yearly trick of looking new
> Is written down in rings of grain.

> Yet still the unresting castles thresh
> In fullgrown thickness every May.
> Last year is dead, they seem to say,
> Begin afresh, afresh, afresh.

It can be the case that the sentences in a poem are—deliberately, when an attentive ear is at work—too much alike to create large-scale drama or challenge the hegemony of meter. In "The Trees," for instance, the syntax is not only highly consonant with the line, parsing it, but predictable, even desultory, containing neither active verbs nor clauses longer than eight metered feet. The periodic sentence in Sonnet 29, with clusters of verb or participial phrases, structures the stanzas and orchestrates the poem. But the "sentence sounds" in "The Trees," those pairs set crosscurrent to the interlocking (abba) rhyme scheme and bisecting each neat quatrain, make only a small ripple on the foregrounded formal surface. In fact, the syntax seems to have been in service to meter from the start.

Larkin makes sure that iambs dominate the opening stanza. Sprinkled throughout, two-syllable words keep a steady ratio between stressed and unstressed syllables—*coming, something, almost, being, recent, relax, greenness.* Monosyllabic words gain or avoid stress according to their grammatical significance—*trees, leaf, buds, kind, grief* (nouns) and *said, spread* (verbs), versus the barely audible function words *(the, are, like, and, their, a, of)*. Meanwhile, the eight-syllable, four-foot line is perfectly consonant with the grammatical chunks of these "normal" orderings, the first one right-branching (lines 1–2), the second heavy with parallelism (lines 3–4). Coupled with hard rhymes that doubly punctuate line and stanza ends, the formal rhythm thoroughly dictates the measured pace and understated tone of Larkin's preferred persona: removed, in command, unflappable.

These same strict patterns will reappear in the third stanza. Again the iambic tetrameter is extremely regular. Again the quatrain is framed by fricatives *(thre / afresh)* and the sentences are predictably distributed, two lines right-branching, then two lines parallel. Also, the stanza's third line mimics faithfully its correlative in stanza 1—same number of syllables, same intransitive verbs, same end-line comma splice between clauses. The pattern-avid human latches on to these similarities happily, along with the dominating metric, a drumbeat supplied by lexical stress *(unresting, castles, fullgrown, thickness, ev'ry, begin, afresh)* and grammatic stress *(thresh, year, dead, seem, say)*. Why would we notice that line 11 is in fact not a compound, like line 3, but hypotactic and inverted, delaying the fundament *(they seem to say)*; that the true comma splice is midline, dividing the two subordinate clauses (what they seem to say); or that we're heading into an imperative in line 12, a departure from the earlier declaratives? Formal pattern mutes the subtle syntactical differences.

In other words, syntax and meter are hardly the matched opponents, duking it out, seen in Sonnet 29. In the Larkin poem, both large- and small-scale rhythms are almost exclusively dictated by line and stanza. One important exception appears in stanza 2, the development section of this sonata. In Sonnet 29, pentameter complicates syntax with an artificial pause at line 11—a crucial enjambment. Here, with the roles reversed, syntax complicates tetrameter by subdividing it, with a two-chunk question and a short, one-chunk answer. For the first time, the vocal phrasing does not conform to the four-foot line:

Is it
that they are born again       and [that] we grow old?
No,
they die too.

Syntax also revises the highly regular iambic pulse. The standard interrogative inversion (verb first) creates an initial trochee, and the balanced subordinate clauses add rhetorical stresses to the opposing pronouns and their respective verbs, stresses reinforced in the next line by the two caesuras and a string of long vowels:

> **Is** it that **they** are **born** a-**gain**
> and **we grow old? No, they die too**.

We can feel the torque added to the music here, and the brusqueness of that very short last sentence. This is a Frostian use of syntax to "put some strain on" the meter, and it enlivens, destabilizes, the poem.

Then the moment is quickly over, and lineation re-asserts control, securing perfect iambs with lexical stress and throwaway function words, and neatly parsing familiar normal declarative:

> Their **year**-ly **trick** of **look**-ing **new**
> Is **writ**-ten **down** in **rings** of **grain**.

But the tone has been altered: an unease has entered the poem at its center, in that balanced, stress-laden line 6, and is recalled by the sibilance of the final stanza *(still, unresting, castles, thresh, thickness, Last, is, seem, say, afresh, afresh, afresh).* After the directness, compression, and muscular spondees of the central independent clause *(**no, they die too**),* the repeating final adverb seems profligate, the trees' instruction to us either flippant or cruel.

Although not as dramatic as Shakespeare's enjambment, Larkin's literally pivotal variation occurs in a context of more rigid formal regularity, and this lengthens its reverberations through the last six lines: the principle is that of the bronze bell. The limitation is also that of the bell: one bold note. In "The Trees," the "sound of sense" remains secondary and can only punctuate, or complicate, or syncopate, the line, never overriding it as we saw in Shakespeare.

Another, more radical strategy is also available for accentual-syllabic poems. Whereas in "The Trees" Larkin used rigorous metric pattern to contain the rhythms of syntax, and to highlight changes in them, in "Cut Grass" he draws on large-scale syntactical phrasing that is vigorous enough to alter the consonant, iambic grid:

Cut grass lies frail:
Brief is the breath
Mown stalks exhale.
Long, long the death

It dies in the white hours
Of young-leafed June
With chestnut flowers,
With hedges snowlike strewn,

White lilac bowed,
Lost lanes of Queen Anne's lace,
And that high-builded cloud
Moving at summer's pace.

There are only two sentences here. The first is made of paired independent clauses yoked by a colon. The first of those clauses, one line long, is four syllables, a compressed simple declarative, two adjectives (*cut* and *frail*) framing the subject *(grass)* and predicate *(lies).* The second clause also uses a copula, or linking verb *(is),* but with its attached modification, all of line 3, it's twice as long. And this time, instead of so-called normal or natural syntactical order, which puts the subject first in the sentence for greatest idiomatic fidelity and greatest discursive clarity, it is inverted. The subject of the sentence is actually *breath.*

Why would Larkin want to do this, other than for the pleasure of that small-scale variation, a way to make line 2 a little different from line 1, just as good musicians never play repeated notes at exactly the same dynamic? Perhaps he is thinking about his next move: his two sentences will be vastly different in length. In order to tether that centrifugal energy, he needs pattern, some similarities between the two, a centripetal force to help the rhyme scheme hold this small lyric together. But those similarities cannot be obvious (since Larkin is never obvious) or boring (Larkin is never boring). And short, simple declarative sentences in normal order carry both the great advantage of extreme clarity and the great risk of boring predictability. By inverting the fundamental subject and its predicate adjective in the second and third independent clauses (lines 2 and 4), he creates a subtle similarity, which is then formally reinforced by the lineation. All four lines in the first stanza can begin with an adjective.

And those adjectives are exactly syntactically parallel in lines 1 and 3 *(cut grass, mown stalks)* and lines 2 and 4 *(brief* and *long)*, rhyming the lines syntactically at their heads as well as literally at their ends. Meanwhile, too, lines 1 and 3 are end-stopped by punctuation. Line 2 isn't punctuated, but it's what I call end-paused: the line "break" appears at a natural division in the syntax, between the independent and the restrictive clauses. And this is just a temporary stay: the sentence completes itself in the very next line, within the rhymed and metered stanza.

Which brings us back to a better reason for the inversion at line 2: it allows an even more radical inversion in its parallel line, line 4, a clause that not only reverses subject and linked modifier but leaves the link out altogether. So syntactically weak, the little copula, so unworthy of utterance. But the pattern implies it clearly enough. Unbeknownst to you, your brain is inferring this grammatically complete assertion, with its curiously transitive subordinate verb: "The death that cut grass dies is long." The inversion and the fixed patterns let Larkin repeat the adjective, delay the subject, elide the predicate, and supply modification far too long and elaborate—the rest of the poem—ever to have been jammed in between subject and weak verb in normal order.

These particular syntactical choices—parallelism, inversion, and elision—have helped to make what seems to me one of the most perfect stanzas in the English language. In a mere sixteen syllables, he gives us four clauses, the syntactical unit of greatest integrity: all of them matched by adjective placement; all of them exactly the same length (four syllables); three of them independent, thus syntactically powerful, two of those paired by inversion. At the same time, masterful small-scale music controls the monosyllabic fabric with full masculine rhyme, dense alliteration of *L* and *S* and *B* sounds, and meter both steady and subtly varied. That compressed opening line encloses two spondees—that is, four stresses in a row, ***Cut grass lies frail****. Line 2 is framed by alliterated stresses, ***Brief*** *is the* ***breath****: falling and then rising, a trochee and an iamb. Line 3 is akin to both: ***Mown stalks*** *ex-****hale*** has the initial spondee of line one, but the closing iamb of line 4. And this arrangement is then repeated—***Long, long*** *the* ***death***—to establish the default position: torqued iambic, each line front-loaded. Pattern, then, in the strict four-syllable, two-foot line, but subtle variation to the pattern, too, in how the stresses are distributed.

But here's what makes the stanza perfect in my mind:

all that pattern, embedded in the syntax, the dimeter, and the rhyme, is overturned by an enormous asymmetry; the tightly unified stanza itself is incomplete, open-ended, unbalanced. A restrictive clause makes its noun specific, "restricts" its meaning. Just as the particular *breath* in line 2 is the one *mown stalks exhale*, the rhyming *death* in line 4 is a particular death, that of cut grass, but we have to go across the stanzaic divide to fetch up that limiting modification. And while the restrictive clause for *breath* encompassed a mere four syllables, this one will span two stanzas and forty-four syllables. Nothing in the symmetrical, balanced, patterned, compressed first three lines has prepared us for this second sentence—technically, a sentence fragment, since the predicate is elided—which is going to barrel past the unified quatrain and blow dimeter right out of the water.

The syntactical strategy at work is the common one noted earlier: right-branching, that gravity-defying tree. One might also imagine a mobile: the fundamental subject and predicate provide the bar from which is hung a modifying word or phrase or clause, and from that another modifier, and so on. It's an efficient way to maintain clarity of reference without inflected endings for our English words. Larkin's highly asymmetrical second sentence is an especially precarious mobile because it hangs not from a fundament but one rung

down, from the restrictive (i.e., subordinate) clause,
and it interlaces its asymmetrical right-branching with
more of the parallelism that opened the poem:

> The death [that] it dies
> > **in** the white hours
> > > **of** young-leafed June,
> > **with** chestnut flowers,
> > **with** hedges snowlike strewn,
> > [with] white lilac bowed,
> > [with] lost lanes of Queen Anne's lace,
> > and [with] that high-builded cloud
> > > moving **at** summer's pace.

Larkin is terribly sly here. With so many prepositions tethered to different spots in the restrictive
clause, some of them placed at the head of the line,
some of them elided for small-scale variation, and each
of their phrases marked by punctuation and end stop
or else end pause, the last of them dangling not even
from the relatively powerful though subordinate predicate *(dies)* but from a participle *(moving)*, it's easy to
misperceive the referents. The five "withs" belong not
to the proximate noun (June), even though the return
to dimeter for two lines would have us think so *(of
**young-leafed June**/with **chest**-nut **flow**-ers)*. Rather,
these phrases are parallel to the initial preposition, *in,*

and thus adverbial: *chestnut flowers, hedges, lilac, Queen Anne's lace,* and *cloud* are all also dying alongside the *mown stalks.*

He didn't leave out prepositions in order to confuse us. We're not confused. Again, parallelism in the syntax and in the lines implies what is missing. Combined with elision, it also gives Larkin, in stanza 3, some stabilizing formal and syntactical similarities to stanza 1: adjective-noun at the head of the line *(Cut grass, Mown stalks, White lilac, Lost lanes);* a return to the default metrical pattern (spondee and iamb—***White lilac bowed***); and another initial spondee, ***Lost lanes,*** "rhymed" by alliteration with the earlier ***Long, long.*** These echoes restore pattern, although not enough, even with end rhyme, to overtake the galloping syntax. Syntax stays in charge of large-scale phrasing, shaping the arc of the poem down the page, conscripting the line to parse the chunks and the stanza to organize them. It is entirely purposeful and masterfully arranged: the substance of what is chunked by the line steadily decreases, from independent clause to subordinate, from clause to prepositional phrase, from prepositional phrase to participial—that is, from central syntactical significance to lesser. The effect is a long diminuendo toward the final elaboration of the cloud, the "briefest" (shortest-lived) item listed.

This structure—this architecture—is the essential drama of the poem's composition, as well as the source of the dynamic shift in tone, from the clipped disinterest of the opening to the final notes of ennui: syntax orchestrates that inexorable movement. Larkin knows this: he is willing to loosen his meter, alternating dimeter and trimeter lines, but he consistently reinforces the syntax by keeping the lines consonant with it, helping us parse the sentence as it opens out. Or rather, opens up: the camera that had focused down at the beginning of the poem, onto the grass at our feet, now points upward, accusingly it seems to me, at the sky, as it does in his great poem "High Windows."

Two rhythmic systems, then, by which to "control the intonations and pauses of the reader's voice," as Frost would have it. In one hand: the power of artifice, the management of the line, and the poet's handy opportunity to tap the reader's hunger for pattern (we are, after all, patternmongering animals) and thereby song. In the other hand: rhythms of syntax, which are embedded in the language itself and used unself-consciously as we translate the world before us: the rhythms of thought, familiar signals to the reader's brain not only for making "meaning" but also for imparting tone. Only in poetry, to its great glory, can we find both systems working at fullest capacity.

# A Varied Pulse

Conventions are tyrannical, and none more so than those regarding form. By now, two lines have been drawn in the sand—requiring either vehement fidelity or vehement opposition to a detectible grid—that few poems try to straddle. What disorients us in Larkin's "Cut Grass" is that one strict metrical pattern is quickly crowded out by another pattern, the poet sowing discord *within* the formal arrangement, casting iamb against spondee, two-foot against three-foot line. But before there was *vers libre,* there was *vers libere,* which found new ways to invigorate the relationship of sentence and line and put syntax in charge of large-scale rhythm. Accentual-syllabic meter was not foresworn but subverted, no longer stable, a fixed grid, but assigned to the moving parts. It often provided a prominent foot without the predictable number of feet in the line; or, a fixed number of scannable feet or accents or syllables without predictable *placement* of stresses among unstressed syllables. This way, the language actually spoken by ordinary human beings, and not an elevated or artificial set of syntax and diction, could be intensified by the echoes of more regular and regulated patterns of song, which we also cherish.

In the early part of the last century, if a poet wanted

the complex nuances and discursive information af-
forded by a complicated syntax, one useful alternative
to enjambment (which had increased and prospered
from Milton forward) was iambic without pentameter,
a pulse set in syntactically consonant lines of varying
length to parse or punctuate the sentences and reinforce
their large-scale vocal phrasing. The opening of Eliot's
"Ash Wednesday" provides a fine example, accompanied
here by Donald Davie's persuasive commentary from
*Articulate Energy:*

1. Because I do not hope to turn again
2. Because I do not hope
3. Because I do not hope to turn
4. Desiring this man's gift and that man's scope
5. I no longer strive to strive towards such things
6. (Why should the aged eagle stretch its wings?)
7. Why should I mourn
8. The vanished power of the usual reign?
9. Because I do not hope to know again
10. The infirm glory of the positive hour
11. Because I do not think
12. Because I know I shall not know
13. The one veritable transitory power
14. Because I cannot drink
15. There, where trees flower, and springs flow, for
    there is nothing again.

Now if we compare lines 8, 10, and 13, it will be observed that 10 and 13 are tied together by an end-rhyme, but that 8 and 10 are tied together no less closely by similarity of grammar. What we have here, in fact, is a sort of parity of esteem between rhyme and metre and grammar or syntax. Every line in the second section, except for the last of all, "rhymes" with some one or more lines in the first section. Thus 9 is linked with 8 by end-rhyme, but . . . 10 no less "rhymes" with 8 by virtue of grammar. 11 rhymes by syntax with 2. 12 rhymes with 3 by virtue of metre and a certain syntactical similarity, but also by syntax with 5 ("Know I shall not know" echoing "strive to strive"). 13 rhymes through 10 with 8. And 14 rhymes, by metre and syntax, with 2.

Eliot's use of iambs should be strict enough to satisfy even Frost, since it is more constant in these fifteen lines than in the fourteen lines of Shakespeare's Sonnet 29. But while Shakespeare was faithful to pentameter and varied the kind of feet that fulfilled it, Eliot largely preserves the kind of foot while varying the number of feet in a given line. In this passage, it is pentameter that shifts, allowing or resisting or flirting with the traditional fixed line length. Meanwhile, the very markers used to observe meter (here, end stop, end pause, and anaphora) chunk the "torrent of notes"

in the periodic sentence and sentence fragment, enabling our perception of the "complex hierarchies" Davie
has analyzed.

With lines so highly consonant with the syntax,
Eliot's poem seems cousin to Lawrence's "Song of the
Man Who Has Come Through." Even though Lawrence
avoids any sort of metrical pulse in the line, any re-
current position of stress among unstressed syllables,
he does maintain a "parity of esteem" among syntactical chunks, "rhyming" through ample lexical repetition
and anaphora. Even if Pound was right—"to break the
pentameter, that was the first heave"—both Eliot and
Lawrence employed a strategy with a distinguished
history: syntactical rhythms more powerful than the
smaller-scale pattern of the line.

In subsequent prosodies, musical phrasing found
additional ways to supersede, yet still refer to, the instrumental grid. In this and the next chapter my examples will include a relaxed accentual pattern, from
Elizabeth Bishop, and from Donald Justice, syllabics both
conventional and jazzed.

*The Moose*

*For Grace Bulmer Bowers*

From narrow provinces
of fish and bread and tea,
home of the long tides

where the bay leaves the sea
twice a day and takes
the herrings long rides,

where if the river
enters or retreats
in a wall of brown foam
depends on if it meets
the bay coming in,
the bay not at home;

where, silted red,
sometimes the sun sets
facing a red sea,
and others, veins the flats'
lavender, rich mud
in burning rivulets;

on red, gravelly roads,
down rows of sugar maples,
past clapboard farmhouses
and neat, clapboard churches,
bleached, ridged as clamshells,
past twin silver birches,

through late afternoon
a bus journeys west,
the windshield flashing pink,

pink glancing off of metal,
brushing the dented flank
of blue, beat-up enamel;

down hollows, up rises,
and waits, patient, while
a lone traveller gives
kisses and embraces
to seven relatives
and a collie supervises.

Goodbye to the elms,
to the farm, to the dog.
The bus starts. The light
grows richer; the fog,
shifting, salty, thin,
comes closing in.

Its cold crystals
form and slide and settle
in the white hens' feathers,
in the gray glazed cabbages,
on the cabbage roses
and lupins like apostles;

the sweet peas cling
to their wet white string
on the whitewashed fences;

bumblebees creep
inside the foxgloves,
and evening commences.

In the first seven stanzas of Bishop's poem (nine of them are quoted here), line length varies from four to eight syllables, and once each these extremes end the six-line stanza *(comes closing in; and a collie supervises)*. They are clearly variants: nineteen of those forty-two lines have six syllables each, seventeen have five. The first stanza contains only lines of five or six syllables; within them, lexical stress and grammatical significance combine to suggest a varied trimeter, a favorite meter for Bishop:

From **nar**-row **prov**-in-*ces*
of **fish** and **bread** and **tea**,
**home** of the **long tides**
where the **bay** *leaves* the **sea**
**twice** a **day** and **takes**
the **her**-rings **long rides**, . . .

But the next line makes it seem futile to look for a dependable accentual-syllabic measure: from *where if the river*, we can extract only two plausible metric feet. And something else happens in stanza 2: for the second time in the poem, lineation separates the predicate *(takes, meets)* from its direct object, and each time the syntactical override is followed by an end-stopped line.

In stanza 3 there will be an even harder enjambment on a possessive *(veins the flats' /)*, but the entire subsequent stanza will be made of end-stopped lines. The only dependable instrumental grid is, at most, a relaxed accentual measure of three stresses per line; and without strict end pause or end stop for all the lines, the two-stress substitution seems not a competing pattern, as in the entirely consonant "Cut Grass," but a natural variant created by the syntax, the sentence sounds torqued here and there by rhyme.

Syntax is meanwhile reinforced by stanzas, each stanza its own musical phrase that arrives at a "lesser resolution" in the extended musical structure of the poem. Among the poem's twenty-eight sestets, only two will be syntactically open (stanza 16, which enjambs the grandparents from here—the bus—to *Eternity,* and the poem's penultimate stanza). The others correspond to significant syntactical chunks. This relationship is clearly established in the long periodic sentence that opens the poem. Here is its essential grammatical structure:

From narrow provinces . . .
       where the bay leaves . . . and takes the herrings,

      where what-the-river-does
      depends on
         if a . . . or if b . . .

> where . . . sometimes the sun does x,
>      and other [times] the sun does y,

> a **bus journeys west**, . . .

After initial modification with right-branching prepositions *(From . . . of)*, and appositive nouns *(provinces/home)*, there are three parallel subordinate clauses. These are contained in separate stanzas, their grammatical parts chunked together and kept apart from the others. Each uses compound syntax but of differing sorts. The first is the most direct, a subject *(bay)* and a compound predicate *(leaves . . . and takes)*. The second is wonderfully balanced with nesting clauses: the predicate *(depends on)* provides a fulcrum between its subject, itself a compound clause *(if the river enters or retreats . . .)*, and its object, yet another conditional clause whose own predicate *(meets)* has compound, symmetrical objects *(the bay coming in, the bay not at home)*. The third stanza divides in half according to its asymmetrical parts, verb phrases this time, one intransitive *(sets)* and one with modified action and object *(veins / the flats' lavender, rich mud / in burning rivulets)*.

This is an enormously complicated syntax (a computer's grammar check would go berserk), but we follow what is said because the larger (and so far parallel) chunks are clearly marked for us—not by the line, as in

the Lawrence poem, but by the stanza, a formal con-
traption constructed with rhymes as was Sonnet 29.
Again in stanza 4, and again like Shakespeare, Bishop
will use the steady, end-stopped, fixed-length stanza
to delay the independent clause, this time shifting to
another kind of chunk, an asymmetrical list of parallel
prepositional phrases:

> **on** red, gravelly roads,
> **down** rows of sugar maples,
> **past** clapboard farmhouses and neat, clapboard churches,
> > [which are] bleached, ridged as clamshells,
> **past** twin silver birches, . . .

All of this modification is adverbial, preceding and delaying its referent, the fundamental verb *journeys.* And
there is one more adverbial phrase in this series, but
anomalous in stanza 5: *through late afternoon,* which
locates the action not in place but in time. Finally—
finally!—we get the fundament, and with it a lesser or
temporary resolution: *a bus journeys west.*

But although the reader's brain may relax at this
point in its anxious search for subject and predicate,
the sentence is not entirely finished. We'll end the
stanza with a new sort of modification, three participial
phrases:

the windshield **flashing** pink,
          pink **glancing** off of metal,
                    **brushing** the dented flank
                              of blue, beat-up enamel;

The lineation is perfectly consonant here, parsing the grammar for us, and the end-stopped stanza is diligently parsing and containing the larger chunk. With this much stability and clarity in the large-scale rhythm, Bishop can confidently offer two small surprises. First, a return to the prepositions of the meandering fourth stanza but now compressed into a single, compact line: *down hollows, up rises.* Then, the sudden realization that our sentence had a compound predicate: the bus also *waits*—and from this additional verb a new compound clause will be suspended: *While* [1] *a lone traveller gives kisses and embraces to seven relatives and* [2] *a collie supervises.*

Phrasing in music, Jourdain reminds us, "is nothing like meter. For one thing, its markers are more subtle. Where meter presents a regular, mostly predictable succession of emphasized notes, phrasing constantly varies," enabling a "series of distinct musical shapes extending across time." And that series can become the source of structure, in a musical composition or in a poem. However much forward momentum is gained from Bishop's long periodic sentence, so masterfully scored by the loose accentual pulse and the stanzaic clusters, equally important are the syntactical coda that follows that sentence and the huge asymmetry the two movements create. Just when the poem had reached the saturation point for slow-paced, understated sonority, the tone and tempo shift dramatically:

> Goodbye to the elms,
> to the farm, to the dog.
> The bus starts. The light
> grows richer; the fog,
> shifting, salty, thin,
> comes closing in.

A sentence fragment and three short, direct independent clauses. Five end-stopped lines. Five caesuras (the first two stanzas had none). To begin the stanza, the same unrhymed riff as the earlier stanzas (abc), plus a matched and rather jaunty triple-rhythm pair:

> Good**bye** to the **elms**,
> to the **farm**, to the **dog**.

And to complete it, a return to the dominant measure and its chief variant (three and two stresses), with the reprise of the short four-syllable line completing a closure-mongering, end-stopped, hard-rhymed pair (the poem's first):

shifting, salty, thin,
comes closing in.

End rhyme has been an active if sometimes muted participant throughout, and has contributed a great deal to the integrity and independence of the stanzas. Now we can see a structure there as well. Usually, in this opening passage, four of every six lines are rhymed, but the rhyming sounds do not appear dependably at fixed places within the stanza (and even that ratio of 4/6 will be varied later in the poem). We do, however, as with Bishop's accentuals, begin with recognizable pattern in the first two stanzas: abc bdc. By stanza 3, the second half of the scheme is reconfigured in each stanza (bab, dbd, dcd), while that opening run of end sounds (abc) continues. In stanza 6, with the long-awaited syntactical resolution, the rhyme adds a new density to the principle of alternation, with exact feminine rhymes bracketing the related half rhymes, *rises/while/gives/embraces/relatives/supervises.* Following the coda (stanza 7) and the poem's first formal couplet *(thin/in),* Bishop will vary the rhyme scheme even more in the rest of the poem, and this shift is signaled in stanza 8, which contains only three rhymed lines *(crystals/settle/apostles),* as do many of the later stanzas (others have just two, and a few use the same end sound for five lines). Her concern seems less with some overall fixed pattern than with stanzaic coherence and integrity.

For the skeptic in the back of the room, there is persuasive evidence that Bishop was extremely purposeful
with these choices, this prosody, and that she recognized syntax as its primary tool, even in the early stages
of composition. We can look first to an earlier treatment
of the occasion, absent the accentual grid and parsing
stanza, in "Cape Breton":

> A small bus comes along, in up-and-down rushes,
> packed with people, even to its step.
> (On weekdays with groceries, spare automobile parts,
>     and pump parts,
> but today only two preachers extra, one carrying his
>     frock coat on a hanger.)
> It passes the closed roadside stand, the closed
>     schoolhouse,
> where today no flag is flying
> from the rough-adzed pole topped with a white china
>     doorknob.
> It stops, and a man carrying a baby gets off,
> climbs over a stile, and goes down through a small
>     steep meadow,
> which establishes its poverty in a snowfall of daises,
> to his invisible house beside the water.
>
> The birds keep on singing, a calf bawls, the bus starts.
> The thin mist follows . . .

These consonant Lawrentian lines of uneven length can barely contain—much less organize—the huge amount of descriptive detail they chunk together in these declarative, right-branching sentences that hurl themselves toward the paratactic coda of the birds, a calf, the bus, the mist. Concrete detail seems to have been the starting place for "The Moose" as well (specifically, the *lupins like apostles, big gray cabbages,* and *white hens' feathers* that survive in stanza 8 of the finished piece). But for the later, longer poem, even the earliest extant drafts employ a loosely rhymed six-line stanza, and that in turn seems closely allied with a patterned syntax. (Note: crossed-out words are in bold type, handwritten insertions in italics.)

From **the** narrow provinces
of fish and bread and tea,
**the** home of the long tides
where the sea wants to leave the sea        tries leaving
    leaves the sea
**over & over** *twice a day*  , and leaves
ice-cakes

from **the** clapboard**ed** farmhouses

white-washed palings
and salt fog on the cabes
**and lupins tall as towers**    **apostles**

> and lupins like apostles
> hailed the bus with
> came out and hailed the bus
> with an    *old*   port lantern      port-side
> **and the old** collie supervised      & climbed aboard ,
> and gave his   approval   last

The next several drafts try to sketch the narrative skeleton, but the poet interrupted herself over and over by tinkering:

> half-seen    faint moonshine and smell of moose and
>     gasoline

> faint moonshine half seen
> a **sharp** smell of moose, an acrid
> smell of gasoline—*a dim*

> **a dim** smell of moose, *an acrid*
> **an acrid**
> smell of gasoline.

She was apparently working out the small-scale rhythms, shaping the lines toward the loose accentual pattern she would settle on.

Over the next dozen drafts, Bishop worked alternatively on various sections, and the handwritten draft 14 focuses on—and numbers—the first five stanzas, re-copied to draft 16. There, she nailed down not only line and stanza but, along with them, a controlling syntax and overall structure for the poem:

1. From narrow provinces
   of fish & bread & tea
   home of the long tides
   where the bay leaves the sea
   twice a day and takes
   the herrings long rides,

2. where if the river
   enters or retreats
   in a wall of brown foam
   depends on if it meets
   the bay coming in,
   the bay not at home;

3. where, silted red,
   the sun sometimes sets
   facing a Red Sea,
   **and** *at* others, veins the flats'
   lavender (rich)[moved with an arrow
      to the head of the line] mud
   **with** burning rivulets;

4. **down** *on* red gravelly roads,
   past rows of sugar maples,
   past clapboard farmhouses
   **and** neat clapboard churches,
   bleached, rigid as clamshells,
   past twin silver-birches,

5. through *the* late afternoon
   a bus **meanders** *journeys* west,
   its windshield **flushed** *flashing?* pink,
   pink flashing off of metal,
   brushing a dented flank
   of blue, beat up enamel;

6. [large blank space]

7. down hollows, up rises,
   to wait, patient, while
   a lone _raveler [sic] gives
   **some** kisses and embraces
   to seven relatives
   and **the** a collie supervises.

There are more large blank spaces, numbered 8 and 9, and a place held in the overall structure, at the end of the clause and the stanza, for those initiating cabbages and lupins:

10. *& the* fog's round crystals
    form and slide and settle
    *in the white hens' feathers,*
    *in the gray glazed cabbages,* [these two lines
       reversed by arrows]
    on the cabbage roses
    and lupins like apostles,

Unlike Kunitz, whose braided rhythm announced itself in generative early lines, Bishop had to discover hers through trial and error, much tinkering, much listening. As with Kunitz, Bishop's attention to small syntactical chunks was crucially enabling to that rhythm, supplying a flexible underlying grid or pulse that allowed delicate syntactical complication. Looking at the documents, we can reasonably surmise that the interplay between large-scale and small-scale systems—as with musical composition—prompted, shaped, refocused, or reinforced the "complex hierarchies" of the piece as it emerged through slow, patient drafting. What directed that interplay in Bishop's magnificent poem was syntax.

# Another Way to Count

If "the living part of a poem is the intonation entangled somehow in the syntax idiom and meaning of a sentence," as Frost insisted, it is not surprising that purely quantative verse—the most mathematically exact grid—has not enjoyed in our poetry a long and distinguished history comparable to that of other languages. Even our lexicon is stress dependent, and as an uninflected language English relies heavily on chunking—its own rhythmic patterns embedded in the syntax. But even though it remains essentially unheard, syllabics can sometimes supply a stable, formal construct while bringing syntactical rhythms to the foreground and increasing their power. Within that discipline, the poet's choices remain the same: whether to make prominent the small-scale arrangements of the line, as Kunitz does in "King of the River," and Lawrence does not; and whether to reinforce the musical phrasing of the syntax with a highly consonant line and even stanza (as Bishop does) or set it in counterpoint through enjambment. Donald Justice seems to want all of these options at once:

## To the Hawks

*McNamara, Rusk, Bundy*

Farewell is the bell
Beginning to ring.

The children singing
Do not yet hear it.

The sun is shining
In their song. The sun

Is in fact shining
Upon the schoolyard,

On children swinging
Like tongues of a bell

Swung out on the long
Arc of a silence

That will not seem to
Have been a silence

Till it is broken
As it is breaking.

There is a sun now
Louder than the sun

Of which the children
Are singing, brighter,

Too, than that other
Against whose brightness

Their eyes seem caught in
The act of shutting.

The young schoolteacher,
Waving one arm in

Time to the music,
Is waving farewell.

Her mouth is open
To sound the alarm.

The mouth of the world
Grows round with the sound.

Competing patterns of music, large-scale and small, dominate this poem. It opens with a syntactically closed couplet, one line end-paused, one line end-stopped.

The two dimeter lines are an exactly matched metrical pair of rising feet (iamb then anapest), and the halving of each line is reinforced by internal rhyme:

> Fare-**well** is the **bell**
> Be-**gin**-ning to **ring**.

This little marvel is followed by another closed, consonant, dimeter couplet:

> The **chil**-dren **sing**-ing
> Do **not** yet **hear** it.

In these two lines, also end-paused and then end-stopped, a slightly different metric is cloned, producing two feminine (unstressed) endings. Meanwhile, the two initial and quite independent couplets have been linked, in lines 2 and 3, with end rhyme, and linked to the next couplet as well:

> Be**ginning** to **ring**.

> The childr**en singing** . . .

> The su**n** is shi**ning**
> **In** their so**ng**. The su**n** . . .

But this new couplet is substantially different from the others, and not only because it is open, not self-enclosed

by syntax. This time, the metrical match is also linking, not self-enclosed: line 5, end-paused, has the same
number and position of stresses as lines 3 and 4, but
line 6 has an initial anapest and a caesura. The caesura
creates the first midline pause in the poem, isolates one
more key word, *sun,* and then, with the lexical sounds
established, lets the rhyming syllables loose into a startling mitosis, generating couplet after linked couplet
down the page:

> sun is shining In song sun is in shining Upon school
> On children swinging tongues bell Swung on long
> silence will been silence Till is broken is breaking.

An enormous amount of lexical repetition and rhyme
dominates the rest of the poem, too—of the poem's
thirty-two lines, a repeating or rhymed word ends all but
six (or, if we allow a liberal definition of rhyme for effects
such as *seem to/music, brighter/brightness,* and *school-
yard/schoolteacher,* all but two: *hear it* and *the world*).
When we also factor in the internal rhyme, repeating
words, and alliteration *(s, sh, sk, sw, b, br),* it's hard to
imagine a sonic texture cohering more completely and
densely than this one, unless it's by Hopkins.

So much formal pattern can paralyze a poem, even
though almost all possible variations of a two-foot line
enliven Justice's five-syllable units. These variations
certainly provide interesting musical complications of

individual lines or couplets—but these very small chunks do very little for the forward momentum of the poem down the page. The source of propulsion is the syntax, and something else happens with that anomalous third couplet. The wonderful initial symmetry of the poem resembles those famous short, dramatically "marked" phrases that open Beethoven's Fifth Symphony and, as the piece unfolds, are swept up into a bigger chunk, an overarching longer phrase. So, too, in this poem. After his two perfectly matched declarative sentences, each two lines long, Justice double-stitches with direct repetition *(The sun is shining, The sun is in fact shining)*, ignores the syntactical integrity of both the line and the stanza, and follows the poem's shortest sentence (eight syllables) with the poem's longest (fifty-two syllables):

> The sun is (in fact) shining   [shining where?]
>     Upon the schoolyard,
>         On children   [which children?]
>             Swinging like tongues   [what kind of tongues?]
>                 Of a bell   [which bell?]
>                     Swung out   [swung out where?]
>                         On the long arc   [which arc?]
>                             Of a silence . . .

Unstoppable, right-branching, alternating prepositional and participial phrases, the sentence muscles through the short lines toward its final subordinate clauses, conscripting the small-scale rhythm however it wishes to create at line 10 another syntactically open (though end-paused) couplet *(Like tongues of a bell)* and at line 11 spill into the poem's first hard initial stress *(Swung)* and the first of two clear and violent enjambments *(the long / Arc of a silence // That will not seem to / Have been a silence).*

Like Beethoven's exposition of his opening theme, this is a kind of runaway horse, the syntax galloping toward the poem's first restrictive clause *(That will not seem to / Have been a silence).* It does not rest until it reaches the poem's first compound: an end-stopped couplet tightly "rhymed" by syntax, meter, direct repetition, and alliteration, and placed exactly at the poem's halfway mark:

Till it is broken
As it is breaking.

Justice was also a composer of music and knew full well the arc created when a piece, as Jourdain says,

wanders into unfamiliar territory then returns to momentary repose. Upon hearing this resolution, a brain groups the preceding notes, then readies itself to perceive the next progression. Lesser resolutions create lesser phrases that can be built into hierarchies of larger ones.

This tight couplet offers a lesser resolution, a place to pause after that asymmetrical, hypotactic fourth sentence. It completes the rushing repetition of the original key words *(sun, children, singing)* and metaphor *(bell, ring, singing, hear, song, tongues, bell, silence* and now *louder, singing)*. Then, after that brief respite, the poem pushes off again into the secondary imagery *(shining, brighter, brightness, eyes)* in another rhyming set *(Louder, brighter, other, schoolteacher)*. This time the long hypotactic sentence is built on parallel elided clauses ([which is] *louder,* [which is] *brighter*). One can conjecture how many paratactic declaratives would be required for its literal translation; instead, prepositions *(than, of, against)* introduce relative pronouns *(which, whose)* and subordinate clauses *(children are singing, Their eyes seem caught)* in an elaborate mobile strung from the truly weak little bar of our common inversion, the expletive *(There is a sun)*. This is fearless hypotaxis and compression. The sentence also wreaks several even more forceful variations in the line as it charges down the page: most notably, the caesuras in lines 20 and 21 *(are singing, brighter, // Too, than that other . . .),* and the enjambment of line 23, which violates the natural chunking of the idiom: *caught in // the act . . .*

But we've made the significant turn back toward the barn—Justice is not interested, as Larkin is in "Cut Grass," in open-ended structure. Sentence 5 is forty syllables, shorter than the one preceding it, and that number will be halved in sentence 6 and then halved again. And sentence 6 will cause only one significant disturbance in the formal arrangements. After the clustered stresses, three of them now *(The **young schoolteach**-er, **Wa**-ving **one arm** in)*, we meet another violent enjambment, another idiomatic grammatical chunk *(in time)* divided across both line and stanza. This awkwardly forces the couplet open, creating tension that is then resolved by the end of the sentence, the return to two stresses and end stop, the closing of the next couplet, and the reintroduction of the poem's first word:

The **young schoolteach**-er,
**Wa**-ving **one arm** in

**Time** to the **mu**-sic,
Is **wa**-ving fare-**well**.

But even this small degree of formal asymmetry is too much for Justice's classicism. Itself a bell, that recurring word becomes a pivot for a final run of direct repetition and connective rhyme as dense as the opening: *waving/ arm/waving/mouth/sound/alarm/mouth/round/sound.* Closure then gets hammered down with tremendous finality in two closed couplets. These comprise two ten-syllable declarative sentences, four perfectly consonant lines that seem to reproduce—and rearrange—the poem's opening meter, syntactical chunks, and balanced internal rhyme:

> Her mouth is open
> To sound the alarm.
>
> The mouth of the world
> Grows round with the sound.

Unlike Larkin's "Cut Grass," which opens up and out, this poem forms an enclosed loop, like the Greek symbol for infinity—an apt emblem for the lyric that stops time, holding in its own music the children, the teacher, and the world all *caught in / The act* of one incomprehensible, world-destroying moment. It is a structure built with the small-scale musical patterns waiting within a purely quantitative measure, but with syntax in charge of that construction.

Justice was a consummate craftsman with an exquisite ear. He was also a formalist through and through, and among his masterful villanelles, sonnets, an oxymoronically arresting sestina, and other received forms, there appear some remarkable syllabic poems (largely concentrated in his second book, *Night Light*, 1965). As I have noted, although it is highly compatible with French (which Justice translated) and other languages, a purely quantitative measure bears no inherent musical relation to English, which relies on stress, in its words and word order, for function and meaning. But in Justice's hands, a fixed syllabic line length can resemble Shakespeare's handling of meter with an even less detectable grid: choosing a very short line, he then teases us with almost every possible arrangement of the stresses available in those small chunks. The effect is something like the opening riffs of jazz improvisation: before the piece settles into recognizable melody and the drum or bass picks up a steady beat, we're not quite sure what tune is being played, what measure or key or tempo.

And when, like jazz, the vocal rhythm of a poem also syncopates the instrumental grid with frequent and even violent enjambment, large-scale musical phrasing is even more necessary to supply structure, coherence, pattern, and variation. A second Justice poem shows what happens when the stable element of "The Moose" and "To the Hawks"—that is, a highly consonant relationship between line, stanza, and sentence—is destabilized. Predictability, the hallmark of pattern, is confounded, leaving our formalist poet only the silent syllabic grid, metrical fragments, and whatever recurrences are available in syntax and lexicon.

*For the Suicides*

*in memory: J & G & J*

If we recall your voices
As softer now, it's only
That they must have drifted back

A long way to have reached us
Here, and upon such a wind
As crosses the high passes.

Nor does the blue of your eyes
(Remembered) cast much light on
The page ripped from the tablet.

****

Once there in the labyrinth,
You were safe from your reasons.
We stand, now, at the threshold,

Peering in, but the passage,
For us, remains obscure; the
Corridors are still bloody.

****

What you meant to prove you have
Proved: we did not care for you
Nearly enough. Meanwhile the

Bay was preparing herself
To receive you, the for once
Wholly adequate female

To your dark inclinations;
Under your care the pistol
Was slowly learning to flower

In the desired explosion,
Disturbing the careful part
And the briefly recovered

Fixed smile of a forgotten
Triumph; deep within the black
Forest of childhood that tree

Was already rising which,
With the length of your body,
Would cast the double shadow.

****

The masks by which we knew you
Have been torn from you. Even
Those mirrors, to which always

You must have turned to confide,
Cannot have recognized you,
Stripped, as you were, finally.

At the end of your shadow
There sat another, waiting,
Whose back was always to us.

                    ****

When the last door had been closed,
You watched, inwardly raging,
For the first glimpse of your selves
Approaching, jangling their keys.

Musicians of the black keys,
At last you compose yourselves.
We hear the music raging
Under the lids we have closed.

In this lyric suite, each section is an independent
structure, arranged first in three stanzas, then two,

then six, then three again, and finally two. The first section suggests an underlying three-beat accentual pattern for the lines:

**If** we re**call** your **voic**es
As **soft**er **now**, it's **on**ly
That they **must** have **drift**ed **back**

A **long way** to have **reach**ed us
**Here**, and upon **such** a **wind**
As **cross**es the **high pass**es.

**Nor** does the **blue** of your **eyes**
(Re**mem**bered) **cast much light** on
The **page ripped** from the **tab**let.

Others might find iambic trimeter here, but if so it is thoroughly destabilized by the "extra" syllable at lines' ends: six of the nine lines have feminine endings, four of them compelled by lexical stress. What we hear—what controls the organization of sounds—is syntactical rhythm, lightly end-paused but cast against the line in two very hard enjambments: *to have reached us / Here,* and *cast much light on / The page.* These are the significant chunks:

> If we recall your voices as softer now,
> it's only
> that they must have drifted back a long way to have
>     reached us here,
> and upon such a wind as crosses the high passes.
>
> Nor does the blue of your eyes, remembered,
> cast much light on the page ripped from the tablet.

Both sentences are unusual. In the first, the casual fundament *(it's)* is a fulcrum between the introductory restrictive clause *(If we . . .)* and the compound nominative, which contains two additional subordinate clauses, one extended and one compressed. The second sentence inverts pieces of the fundament (blue does not cast much light . . .). And the two end-stopped sentences have a formal relationship as well: the second is exactly half as many lines and syllables as the first.

The next section is also made of two sentences, but the shorter one is placed first. And while most of section 1 was hypotactic, this one is fiercely parallel. After introductory modification in the first line, we are given four normal-order, independent clauses: *you were safe . . . , we stand . . . , the passage remains . . . , the corridors are . . .* But only the first of these rhythmic chunks is offered whole, contained by the line *(You were safe from your reasons).* Each of the others is stuttered out, interrupted by punctuation, modifiers, end stops, and one extremely violent enjambment that follows a caesura and isolates an insignificant function word:

> We stand, now, at the threshold,

> Peering in, but the passage,
> For us, remains obscure; the
> Corridors are still bloody.

With five of the six lines end-stopped, a powerful small-scale rhythm contends with the syntax, chunking it into smaller pieces. Something also contends with the implied measure. We can still locate three plausible stresses in each seven-syllable line but can be confident in most lines only of two—and sometimes suspect there are four—

> We **stand**, *now,* at the **thresh**old . . .

> **Cor**rid*ors* are **still blood**y.

Unease is creeping into the tone.

It arrives full blown in section 3. Before we get the polysyllabic words with their dependable, lexical ratio of stresses *(**Near**-ly e-**nough. Mean**-while),* there is first a string of monosyllabic words, with no compelled distribution (or even amount) of stress; inverted syntax (predicate object placed first); another enjambment that splits the predicate; and the use of line chunk to unbalance the balanced sentence:

> What you meant to prove you have / Proved:
> we did not care for you / Nearly enough.

Then the poem's hardest enjambment, across both line and stanza *(Meanwhile the // Bay)*, initiates a compound sentence composed of parallel and then right-branching clauses. This sentence is also hesitant, stuttered out in curious small inversions or interruptions:

> the for once / Wholly adequate female . . .
> the briefly recovered // Fixed smile . . .
> deep within the black / Forest of childhood
> that tree // Was already rising which, / With the
>     length of your body, / Would cast . . .

Initial stresses *(Proved, Nearly, Bay, Wholly, Under)* have been largely replaced by a rising rhythm *(To **receive**, To your **dark**, In the de**sired**, Dis**turb**ing the **careful part**.* Twice, the passage even suggests plausible anapestic dimeter—

> And the **brief**-ly re-**cov**-er'd . . .
> With the **length** of your **bod**-y, . . .

and it comes to rest on an iambic trimeter line.

Would **cast** the **dou**-ble **shad**-ow.

The language of metrics is useful in describing the number and kind of small-scale musical variations in this poem—all the possible relationships of stressed and unstressed syllables available in seven candidates, without neglect of semantic and emotive meaning. Justice knew his Shakespeare. This is, however, a very long way from accentual-syllabic measure. If there is any rhythmic *pattern* in the line, rather than a strict syllabic count, about all that can be said firmly is that most of the lines tend to make a small arc, rising at the outset, falling at their close. The feminine ending is asserted over and over, in each section, by enjambment *(you have / Proved; reached us / Here; the / Corridors)* and lexical stress *(recovered, explosion, flower, pistol, female, bloody, tablet)*. In the next section, it will, as in the opening section, dominate. Eight of the nine lines end without a stress, some of them tossing away the objective case pronouns *(we **knew** you, can**not** have **rec**ognized you, Whose **back** was **always to** us)*. Similarly, the lines dependably open on an iamb or anapest *(The **masks**, Have been **torn**, Those **mir**rors, At the **end**, Whose **back**)*. Only one line uncontrovertibly varies the paradigm:

**Stripp'd**, as you **were**, finally.

The others, whatever their number of clear stresses or scannable feet, rise and then fall, like so many of the earliest lines.

And the section itself makes an arc. This time, there are three sentences whose structures overlap. The first is the shortest, with interruptive modification between subject and verb *(masks . . . have been torn).* The second, the longest, employs a similar but longer interruption *(to which . . . confide),* and also attaches a final subordination *(as you were).* The third sentence elaborates also at its end *(waiting, / Whose back was always to us).*

This third sentence also appears alone in its own stanza—like the third stanza of section 1—and that coincidence also applies to the rhythmic echoes, the "arcing" line, the steady end stop and end pause, and the "rhyming" first-person plural pronouns *(If we . . . to us)* for a quietly effective closure. But this closure is only a "lesser" resolution: the poem has a coda, yet another section. In it, for the first time, the stanzas are not tercets but two quatrains. For the first time, every line is at least end-paused—that is, grammatically chunked. Six of the eight lines are also emphatically end-stopped with punctuation; and only two of the lines have feminine endings *(raging).* This makes a clearly discernible pattern of rising rhythm, reinforced by initial iambs in every instance except the final line:

**Un**-der the **lids** we have **closed**.

The two stanzas of this last section are not only welded together by mirroring end words. Each is organized around an extended metaphor drawn from the same lexical source: the keys to the locked door, and the keys on the piano. Meaning pulls us in two different directions, even as the repeated source word yokes the two stanzas in an interlocking couplet:

Approaching, jangling their keys.

Musicians of the black keys, . . .

There is other blind-stitching: *last door/first glimpse/at last,* and *jangling/we hear/music.* Even more startling, however, is how the two stanzas are both tied together and set against one another by two more puns. There is no mistaking them or their structural importance. The first of these *(compose)* rhymes with an end word *(closed)* and redefines the raging music as the last we hear of the "voices" that opened the poem. The second pun *(lids)* completes—resolves—both the piano imagery of stanza 2, and the human eyes of stanza 1 *(watched, glimpse)* and section 1, while suggesting yet another reference: coffin lids. This is density of a different order than what we've had in the poem so far, and Justice structures it with syntax: he divides the last stanza in half with the poem's shortest two sentences, using the line to parse them, letting the images accrue and resonate. The first sentence, given over wholly to the "you" of the title and dedication, is kept syntactically independent from the second sentence's plural first person, making the clauses in the last declarative seem utterly bereft and the formal playfulness of the piece movingly desperate.

A great jazz musician needs a group, a trio, a partner instrument to maintain the ghost of the pulse against which the idiosyncratic improvisations can occur. It is the counterpoint that we respond to. Here, too, the technical prowess is not meant to dazzle. Both the riffs and the subtle, all-but-erased grid are essential to the poem's rich emotional fabric. Both serve as necessary and appropriate expressions of a complicated grief.

# Off the Grid

After detailed analysis of a poem, someone usually asks whether all that has been pointed to—or any of it, for that matter—was *intended* by the poet. The truthful answer seems weaselly: yes and no. It's probably not often an authentic poem of "felt thought" emerges solely from a willfulness intent on all the effects I have identified, any more than studying your feet as they move will help you down the stairs. But the mirrors in the ballet studio have a purpose: neither a first-position plié nor skillful iambic pentameter occurs spontaneously in the human animal.

The making of a poem is not a performance but an adventure, an act of discovery. Most poets of high formal appetite often do perceive, in advance of the concrete materials of the poem, some shape or heft or tone or set of means—what Susanne Langer calls a "formal apprehension." It influences countless choices in the drafting process: this word instead of that one, this lineation or syntax, this length and order of stanzas. When the poet releases the poem to readers, she in essence ratifies those sometimes instinctive, sometimes fretted-over preferences, small or large, and their impact on the poem has been accepted, owned, *intended* through that final act. The more alert and experienced the poet, the more numerous those options have been, whether in the heat of composition or in later revision, whether self-conscious or intuitive. The intuition, after all, was tutored by the many poems the poet had previously read and written, their many choices.

Without seeing the drafts of "For the Suicides," as we can so much of Bishop's work, we lack evidence of willfulness about, say, metrical variation. And nothing would have been resolved by querying Justice, who was a sly, ironic, private man. But we can look at the syntax that rearranges the default position of speech, for instance, and ask why the poet invited or seized on that opportunity and those effects. Why, instead of presenting straightforward declarative, "Now we stand at the threshold," did Justice insert punctuated interruption—*We stand, now, at the threshold*— if not to slow and roughen the line with two caesuras and juxtaposed stresses? Or why, since the adverb could appear with clarity and emphasis anywhere in the clause—

to which you always must have turned . . .
to which you must always have turned . . .
to which you must have always turned . . .
to which you must have turned, always—

why is it placed early, awkwardly, stranded at the end of the line and stanza—*to which always // you must have turned . . .*—if not to guarantee falling rhythm with a lexical trochee, a feminine ending? It doesn't matter whether the analytical left brain decides, or the "intuitive" right brain: both belong to the poet. And both are equally engaged when patterned line or stanza conflict with the phrasing of the syntax. Consider this:

> Meanwhile the bay, the female, for once wholly adequate to your dark inclinations, was preparing herself to receive you; the pistol was slowly learning under your care to flower in the desired explosion.

Grammatical, yes; vital, no. All writing, Frost said, is only as good as it is dramatic, and Justice's vital, lineated sentence dramatizes the two suicides, the bay in one tercet, the pistol in another, *dark inclinations* jammed up against *care, to flower* left resonant at the end of line and stanza before a new stanza delivers the outcome, *the desired explosion.* Did Justice plan in advance to place the actual deaths at the poem's center? Did he simply happen to narrate them that way? Or, did he, in draft number 8 or 15 or 22, excise or reposition a tercet in order to maneuver those events to the center? Would he be surprised (with Justice, this is unlikely) to learn they appear at the center? Does an answer change the impact of their placement, recognized or intuited by the reader? Since the impact is not lessened when the reader is analytical rather than intuitive in one of her myriad visitations to the poem, wouldn't the poet's own understanding of the poem be clarified, intensified, by some understanding of what created it?

"The ear does it," Frost said. "The ear is the only true writer and the only true reader." But he certainly didn't mean the ear should be left untrained, saying that "I . . . have *consciously* set myself to make music out of what I may call the sound of sense" (my emphasis). He also said, "The possibilities for tune from the dramatic tones of meaning struck across the rigidity of a limited meter are endless":

> it reminds me of a donkey and a donkey cart; for some of the time the cart is on the tugs and some of the time on the hold-backs. You see it's that way all the time. The one's doing that and the other—the one's holding the thing back and the other's pushing it forward—and so on, back and forward.

For Frost, the push-pull happens primarily *within* the line, which in his poems is almost always consonant as well as metered, reinforcing the same syntactical chunks we hear in speech and thereby replicating idiom. In his view, syntax helps establish and then "ruffle[s] the meter," never overturning it. Some of his well-known poems begin like this:

**Some**thing there **is** that **does**n't **love** a **wall**,
That **sends** the **fro**zen-**ground**-**swell un**der **it**,
And **spills** the **up**per **boul**ders *in* the **sun**;
And **makes gaps** even **two** can **pass** a**breast**.

\*

**Ma**ry sat **mu**sing on the **lamp**-**flame** at the **ta**ble
**Wait**ing for **War**ren. *When* she **heard** his **step**,
She **ran** on **tiptoe** *down* the **dark**ened **pass**age
To **meet** him *in* the **doorway** *with* the **news**
And **put** him *on* his **guard**. "**Si**las is **back**."

\*

*There is* a **sing**er **every**one has **heard**,
**Loud**, a **mid**-**sum**mer and a **mid**-**wood bird**,
Who **makes** the **sol**id **tree trunks sound** a**gain**.

For Frost, the dominant rhythm of English speech is either "strict iambic or loose iambic." "To furnish the variety in relation of my tines to it," creating an idiomatic "tune," he sets lexical trochees at the beginnings *(**Some**-thing, **Ma**-ry, **Wait**-ing)* and ends of lines *(ta-ble, **pass**-age),* juxtaposes stresses midline *(**makes gaps, mid-wood bird, tree trunks sound**),* and occasionally makes lines of more than ten syllables. The consonant metric line also pays dividends: invited to look for pattern, we find it, and accord either a metrical stress or, softer, a durational (pyrrhic) foot (these are italized in the quoted stanzas) to unstressed function words. So when he says, "[t]he meter is just as rigid as two crossed swords in the Sword Dance," he means the *number* of feet per line, in a line sometimes full of variants. Iambs are much more dominant in Larkin's "Cut Grass," but because of its struggle between two- and three-beat lines, Frost probably would have dismissed it as he did all "free verse."

But "free" verse poems have, over the past century, carried his fidelity to "the sound of sense" into other equally effective prosodies, allowing large-scale syntactical rhythms to dictate, dominate, or alter a less predictable even if more strictly quantitative "grid." In "To the Hawks" and "For the Suicides," Justice uses an unvaried syllabic count that the stresses "dance around." In "The Moose," Bishop uses a loose accentual pattern. And both poets employ varying degrees of stanzaic pattern, rhyme, and enjambment, to support or syncopate the syntactical phrasing.

For Bishop as for Yeats, a paradigmatic measure and a rhymed stanza enabled composition. For both Bishop and Yeats as mature poets, their first allegiance remained not to that scaffolding but to syntax. This makes their prosodies more similar than one may have assumed to Stanley Kunitz's, which fashions a steady pulse from syntax and consonance in "King of the River." In fact, all the sampled texts so far—whether in rhyme and meter or free verse—have provided strategies for enacting pattern simultaneous with variation. But what about poems, such as Lawrence's "Snake," structured not as lyric but as narrative?

1   A snake came to my water-trough
    On a hot, hot day, and I in pyjamas for the heat,
    To drink there.

2   In the deep, strange-scented shade of the great
        dark carob-tree
    I came down the steps with my pitcher
    And must wait, must stand and wait, for there he
        was at the trough before me.

3   He reached down from a fissure in the earth-wall
        in the gloom
    And trailed his yellow-brown slackness soft-
        bellied down, over the edge of the stone trough
    And rested his throat upon the stone bottom,
    And where the water had dripped from the tap, in
        a small clearness,
    He sipped with his straight mouth,

Softly drank through his straight gums, into his
    slack long body,
Silently.

4   Someone was before me at my water-trough,
And I, like a second comer, waiting.

5   He lifted his head from his drinking, as cattle do,
And looked at me vaguely, as drinking cattle do,
And flickered his two-forked tongue from his lips,
    and mused a moment,
And stooped and drank a little more,
Being earth-brown, earth-golden from the burning
    bowels of the earth
On the day of Sicilian July, with Etna smoking.

6   The voice of my education said to me
He must be killed,
For in Sicily the black, black snakes are innocent,
    the gold are venomous.

7   And voices in me said, If you were a man
You would take a stick and break him now, and
    finish him off.

8   But must I confess how I liked him,
How glad I was he had come like a guest in quiet,
    to drink at my water-trough

And depart peaceful, pacified, and thankless,
Into the burning bowels of this earth?

9  Was it cowardice, that I dared not kill him?
10  Was it perversity, that I longed to talk to him?
11  Was it humility, to feel so honoured?
12  I felt so honoured.

13  And yet those voices:
    *If you were not afraid, you would kill him!*

14  And truly I was afraid, I was most afraid,
    But even so, honoured still more
    That he should seek my hospitality
    From out the dark door of the secret earth.

15  He drank enough
    And lifted his head, dreamily, as one who has
        drunken,
    And flickered his tongue like a forked night on the
        air, so black,
    Seeming to lick his lips,
    And looked around like a god, unseeing, into the
        air,
    And slowly turned his head,
    And slowly, very slowly, as if thrice adream,
    Proceeded to draw his slow length curving round
    And climb again the broken bank of my wall-face.

16  And as he put his head into that dreadful hole,
    And as he slowly drew up, snake-easing his
        shoulders, and entered farther,
    A sort of horror, a sort of protest against his
        withdrawing into that horrid black hole,
    Deliberately going into the blackness, and slowly
        drawing himself after,
    Overcame me now his back was turned.

17  I looked round, I put down my pitcher,
    I picked up a clumsy log
    And threw it at the water-trough with a clatter.

18  I think it did not hit him,
    But suddenly that part of him that was left behind
        convulsed in undignified haste,
    Writhed like lightning, and was gone
    Into the black hole, the earth-lipped fissure in the
        wall-front,
    At which, in the intense still noon, I stared with
        fascination.

19  And immediately I regretted it,
    I thought how paltry, how vulgar, what a mean act!

20  I despised myself and the voices of my accursed
        human education.

21　And I thought of the albatross,
　　And I wished he would come back, my snake.

22　For he seemed to me again like a king,
　　Like a king in exile, uncrowned in the underworld,
　　Now due to be crowned again.

23　And so, I missed my chance with one of the lords
　　Of life.

23　And I have something to expiate;
　　A pettiness.

In *The Birth of Tragedy,* Nietzsche reminds us that the Greeks honored two gods of art: Apollo, god of light and reason, order and clarity; and Dionysus, god of wine and orgy, chaos and life force. D. H. Lawrence is nothing if not Dionysian, a lifelong apostle of life force and asymmetry: that's the thematic burden of most of what he wrote (including this poem—the snake does live in a black hole). We can see it first—and Lawrence makes this easy by assigning each sentence, with exceptions, its own closed stanza—in the tremendous variety of sentence length. This makes what Jourdain calls, describing music, a "series of highly irregular sonic shapes" across and down the page. After Justice's careful paradigms of line and stanza, the syntax here seems at first inchoate, unchecked, a centrifugal force.

But there are restraints aplenty, and a different kind of pattern, also supplied by the syntax. For instance, nothing is more orderly, predictable, and Apollonian than a list, and a long compound sentence with multiple predicates, like sentence 3, is a list. In the poem's first extended series of actions, the snake *reached, trailed, rested, sipped, drank.* This is already muscular— four more predicates than required to make a clause, the most powerful unit of syntax. But in addition, usually intransitive verbs, *trailed* and *rested,* are here made more active (and powerful) by giving them direct objects *(trailed his . . . slackness, rested his throat).* These are then followed by usually transitive verbs, *sipped* and *drank,* set in edgy tension when their direct object (water) is elided, withheld. And this syntactical vigor is underscored by putting those verbs all in the same prominent position, at the heads of the lines.

Apollo (and Justice) would approve, but Lawrence makes sure those anaphoric verbs also thrust into right-branching limbs of different lengths, each verb phrase rhythmically different from the others and reinforced by the consonant lineation:

> He reached down from a fissure in the earth-wall in
> the gloom

> And trailed his yellow-brown slackness soft-bellied
> > down, over the edge of the stone trough
> And rested his throat upon the stone bottom, . . .

The first of these line chunks is fourteen syllables long, the second is twenty, the third only eleven, and the next one—*he sipped with his straight mouth*—will be the shortest, six syllables. This asymmetry envigorates the structurally symmetrical nature of a list.

And there's more subtle variation to come. Halfway through the sentence, and this time before the verb it will modify, Lawrence inserts a subordinate clause *(where the water had dripped from the tap, in a small clearness).* Then he repeats the so-far elided subject pronoun *(**He** sipped . . .),* drops the anaphoric conjunction *(And),* and ends his list with a verb phrase the same syllabic length as the first one:

> Softly drank through his straight gums, into his slack
> > long body, . . .

But Lawrence likes his "lesser resolutions" a little off-balance, so he frames this last verb phrase with adverbs, made obvious by placement at the start of the lines: *Softly . . . Silently.* Thus we get pattern, from the parallel verb phrases, simultaneous with variation, from the length and structure of those phrases. This is what Frost called a vital sentence: it enacts the snake's powerful ease within its body.

There are four of these long compound "action" sentences in the poem, comprising an increasing number of verbs—six of them in sentence 3, eight in sentence 5, and ten in sentence 15—cast into shorter and shorter syntactical chunks. Check out the predicates, and their verb phrases, in sentence 5, the next action stanza:

He lifted his head from his drinking,      (9)
And looked at me vaguely,      (6)
And flickered his two-forked tongue from his lips,      (10)
And mused a moment,      (5)
And stooped      (2)
And drank a little more, . . .      (6)

Varied in lengths—and the list also camouflaged, disguised by a subordinate refrain tacked on to the first two phrases *(as cattle do, as drinking cattle do)*; disguised by lineation, which chunks together *flickered . . . and mused, stooped and drank;* and disguised by the two lines of right-branching modification *(Being earth-brown . . . Etna smoking)* added to the last phrase.

Meanwhile, this snake-action sentence is yoked to the previous one, and to the next one, by the last predicate, *drank a little more . . .* That verb came last in sentence 3

as well—*Softly drank through his straight gums*—but in
15 it will come first, initiating another grocery list of actions, of predicates:

> He drank enough
> And lifted his head . . .
> And flickered his tongue . . .
> And looked around . . .
> And turned his head . . .

All apples—all the same weight and heft and rhythm.
But Lawrence varies them with right-branching adverbial chunks, using the shortest verb phrases to balance
a bulge:

> He drank enough        (4)
> And lifted his head, dreamily, as one who has
>      drunken,        (14)
> And flickered his tongue like a forked night on the
>      air, so black, seeming to lick his lips,        (20)
> And looked around like a god, unseeing,
>      into the air,        (14)
> And slowly turned his head, . . .        (6)

Highly symmetrical, that pattern—and Lawrence won't
rest there. As in sentence 3, he changes the syntactical
arrangement with modification inserted before rather

than after the verb phrase, and to do so he uses his earlier subordinating conjunction:

> And slowly, very slowly, **as** if [he were] thrice
>     adream, . . .

It's a useful delay, a springboard to the longest verb phrase in all three stanzas of snake action:

> Proceeded to draw his slow length curving round /
>     And climb again the broken bank of my wall-face.

Twenty-three syllables right-branching with a new verb form, two concrete infinitives—*to draw . . . and climb*—that energize the abstract predicate, *proceeded.*

Lawrence is not yet through with that conjunction. In sentence 5, it formed a refrain—*as cattle do, as drinking cattle do*—and it will do so again in sentence 16, aggressively, not trailing the phrase but placed at the head of the line, the sentence, and the stanza, delaying the fundament with parallel subordinate clauses:

> And as he put his head into that dreadful hole,
> And as he slowly drew up, snake-easing his shoulders,
>     and entered farther,
> A sort of horror . . .
> Overcame me . . .

The snake now appears in a different kind of sentence—no longer a "natural order" compound but the hypotactic, hierarchical syntax only used so far for the human with his learned behavior.

We can see that behind the variations keeping it lively and plausible, there is a solid architecture in the poem, patterns and repetitions that structure as well as pace the story of man and snake. Like "Cut Grass" and "To the Hawks," that structure is built mainly out of syntax; unlike those poems, its shape is neither a rocket launching off into outer space nor a highly symmetrical ellipse that contains an expansion at its center. Rather, this is large-scale phrasing with a motif. No longer strictly musical, no longer pure lyric that suspends, extends, and examines a moment of intense feeling, "Snake" shoulders a narrative, a movement through time. The poem's plot line is the struggle between thought and action, between civilization and nature, and the two very different kinds of syntax enact that struggle.

If it seems that the snake gets all the long sentences, the speaker the shorter ones, it's not because a snake is long and skinny. As Lawrence's novels predict, it's action—natural, physical, sensual—that usually gets the longer, more sensuous, paratactic or compound sentences. Thought, the "voice of my education," the rational brain of the civilized man, are rendered in the more elaborate, even if shorter, hypotactic sentences. And hypotaxis contains an imbalance of power: one clause is subordinated to the other. In contrast to the snake-action sentences we've been analyzing, consider sentences 8–11:

> But must I confess how I liked him,
> How glad I was he had come like a guest in quiet, to
>     drink at my water-trough
> And depart peaceful, pacified, and thankless,
> Into the burning bowels of this earth?
>
> Was it cowardice, that I dared not kill him?
> Was it perversity, that I longed to talk to him?
> Was it humility, to feel so honoured?

Like all interrogatives, unlike the snake's "natural order," this syntax is inverted. And in that anomalous stanza of syntactically independent lines, sentences 9–11, inversion provides anaphora, lining up three abstractions— *cowardice, perversity, humility*—that will be echoed in the poem's last word: *pettiness.* Notice, too, how subordinate clauses dominate the passage:

> how I liked him,
> how glad I was he had come . . .

that I dared not kill him?
that I longed to talk to him?

Liking him, being glad, longing to talk to him are fine sentiments but not fully embraced here. While the inversion elevates—and rhymes syntactically—the abstractions, the sentiments are left as grammatical objects (what he must confess), then deferred and displaced by a stand-in *(it)*. The offer of empathy that follows in the poem's shortest sentence *(I felt so honoured)* is accomplished with a weak copula for its predicate, at best acharacteristic if not insincere. The speaker does not—and will not—act on the sentiment: the syntax tells us so.

In the poem's first half, half the sentences are short and usually hypotactic. These are the ones controlled by the speaker. Meanwhile, the long, compound snake sentences are full of predicates, of equal, powerful actions:

He lifted his head . . .
And looked at me . . .
And flickered his two-forked tongue . . .
And mused . . .
And stooped and drank . . .

Increasingly, though, even these compound sentences begin to include subordinate clauses, at first coming after but then, intruding, before the verbs until, at sentence 16, the snake no longer has a single independent predicate, much less a string of them:

> And as he put his head into that dreadful hole,
> And as he slowly drew up, snake-easing his shoulders,
>     and entered farther,
> A sort of horror, a sort of protest against his
>     withdrawing into that horrid black hole,
> Deliberately going into the blackness, and slowly
>     drawing himself after,
> Overcame me now his back was turned.

In this last "action stanza," the snake and the speaker are closely juxtaposed structurally and dramatically for the first time. And when that happens, the fundament, the center of power in the sentence and stanza, no longer belongs to the snake but to the "voice of my education": *A sort of horror, a sort of protest . . . overcame me.* The snake gets only subordinate clauses and participial phrases: this is the first significant reversal of the pattern. The second reversal comes in the sentence that follows, where the speaker appears alone, without the snake. Suddenly, forgoing complex syntax in the shortest series of independent, fundament-first, paratactic clauses yet to appear in the poem, the human *acts:*

> I looked round, I put down my pitcher,
> I picked up a clumsy log . . .

There are no anaphoric conjunctions here, no right-branching elaboration by prepositions, no consistent line integrity. Just three independent clauses crammed together, the compound subject not tactfully elided, as in the snake sentences, but closely repeated *(I, I, I)*. And then he conscripts for himself the reptilian right-branching: *And threw it at the water-trough with a clatter.* Clumsy, hasty, brutal. This is the Master of the Natural World in action.

And he *has* mastered it: the syntax tells us this, too. The snake becomes subjunctive and subordinate *(I wished he would come back),* his last active verbs conducted by a restricted nominative *(that part of him that was left behind).* He—the whole he, the whole snake—is now *my snake,* and can only "seem" in one final appearance, a sentence fragment. Our hypotactic guy supplants him, taking up the snake's "natural order" syntax and equalizing conjunction—*and . . . and . . . and*—but he's got only the weaker predicates of mind, stuck up there at the heads of the sentences, syntactically in charge: *I think, I regretted, I thought, I despised, I thought, I wished, I missed, I have.* The very last verb in a poem full of verbs is kept only potential, an infinitive, *to expiate.*

According to Jourdain, "phrasing imparts a kind of narrative to music. It is the mechanism by which a composition can play out a grand drama." And phrasing is the rhythmic system that builds "large-scale musical objects and thereby induc[es] large-scale musical perceptions." Syntactical rhythm, too, even though it "lacks the repetitive, evenly paced accentuations of measured rhythm," can orchestrate "a succession of irregular sonic shapes that combine in various ways like the parts of a painting, sometimes hanging in exquisite balance, sometimes joining forces to gyrate or plunge or swirl." That seems the right description not only of "Snake," which gyrates and swirls more than my previous examples, but all these poems. Lawrence simply relies less on any sort of regularity or detectable grid for his lineation, using syntax instead to manage both small-scale and large-scale rhythms.

That he does so is largely a matter of temperament, as is Larkin's willingness to throw a poem open to radical asymmetry and leave it there, or Justice's need to close the circle. In light of such large and instructive differences, the ongoing spats between "neoformalists" and the writers of free verse, or between "traditional" and "experimental" poets, seem beside the point. Of course, Apollo and Dionysus are well-matched opponents, and the stakes, as with most religions, have been very high: remember Apollo's flaying of Marsyas and the Bacchanals' beheading of Orpheus? Different centuries, different aesthetics have worshipped one more fervently than the other, putting a premium on pattern over variation, or energy over order, or, currently, fragmentation and disjunction over unity and coherence. But despite those priorities and beliefs, great poets petition both deities.

It's true that during the twentieth century, coincident with a greater tolerance for dissonance in all the arts, more room was sought for asymmetry and variation in poetry, but this now seems less a revolution than an evolution of aesthetic intention. And after one hundred years of free verse invention and mastery, contemporary poets need not focus solely on lineation or fall unthinking into one of the dominant conventions of our time: on the one hand, a "sincere" poem made accessible by predictable simple declarative sentences, all about the same length, chunked by end stop and end pause into three or four roughly equivalent short lines; on the other hand, an "edgy" poem of passive predication or no predication at all, sentence fragments torqued by violent enjambments or arranged for a purely visual effect on the page.

Most of us who write poems rather than prose have very high formal appetites. Lineation affords quite evident and audible opportunities for making pattern, and we will and should go on exploring them all. But it's useful to remember that other sorts of pattern are also there for us to use—rhythms inherent to the language we write in, the source of its muscle and sinew and music, its clarity and its resonance and its power.

# Glossary

*Boldface within an entry refers to terms defined else-where in this glossary.*

**Accentual verse**—a poetic **meter** with a fixed number of stressed syllables in every line, no matter the number of unstressed syllables.

**Accentual-syllabic verse**—the most prevalent poetic **meter** in English; measures both a recurring number of syllables in every line and a recurring position of stresses among unstressed syllables.

**Adjective**—a word that **modifies** a **noun**, or whatever functions as a noun, usually appearing adjacent to it (*dumb* bunny, heir *apparent,* roads *north* or *south*) or connected to it by a **linking verb** (Spilling salt is *unlucky,* and she looked *bereft*).

**Adjectival phrase**—a group of words that **modifies** a **noun**. The term indicates function in a sentence and may apply to a **subordinate clause** (the man *I love*) or to grammatical **phrases** (the man *changing a tire,* the man *without qualities*). See **participle** and **preposition**.

**Adverb**—a word that **modifies** a **verb** (Come back *later*), an **adjective** (*piping* hot), a **preposition** (*almost* over the top), or another adverb (running *too* fast); commonly, an adjective converted with the suffix "–ly" *(quickly, softly)*.

**Adverbial phrase**—a group of words that **modifies** an action, usually specifying when, where, why, or how. The term indicates syntactical function and may apply to a **subordinate clause** (I went to town *after I fed the chickens*), or to grammatical **phrases** (No one arrived *on a white horse, shouting my name*). See **preposition** and **participle**.

**Alliteration**—repetition of initial sounds in proximate words (*cool kayak* but not *crunchy celery; every egg* but not *eyeless elephants*); a subset of **rhyme**.

**Anapest**—in **accentual-syllabic verse**, a metrical **foot** placing a stressed syllable after two unstressed syllables, creating **rising rhythm** and **triple meter** when repeated *(in the HOUSE by the SIDE of the ROAD)*.

**Anaphora**—repetition of a word or words at the beginning of adjacent or proximate lines; a form of likeness (to "carry back"); a subset of **rhyme** and refrain (see poems by Whitman).

**Article**—a **modifier** that makes a **noun** generic (**indefinite**—*a* book) or particular (**definite**—*the* book).

**Cadence**—a rhythmic sequence of sounds with recurrence that is recognizable but not necessarily regularized; in poems, rhythmic pattern not organized by **meter**.

**Caesura**—a pause in the line caused by punctuation, letting syntax trump the artificial ("made") rhythm of the line.

**Clause**—a powerful and flexible grammatical unit that contains a **subject** and a **predicate**; may be **independent**, encompassing the **fundament** of the **sentence**, or made **subordinate** by a **pronoun** or **conjunction**; can subsume numerous, less powerful, grammatical **phrases**; can be used as a phrase to **modify** a **noun** or **verb**; can also (less frequently) be used as a noun (*What he did* was wrong). See **restrictive clause**, as well as **complex** and **compound sentences**.

**Closed couplet**—a two-line **stanza** containing a grammatically complete, independent statement and marked ("closed") by punctuation at the end of the second line.

**Complex sentence**—a complete syntactical unit containing at least one **independent clause** and at least one **subordinate clause**.

**Compound**—a pair or a series of equivalent syntactical units (words, **phrases**, or **clauses**) usually joined by a coordinating **conjunction**.

**Compound sentence**—a complete syntactical unit containing more than one **independent clause**.

**Conjunction**—a word that unites pairs or multiple members of a series (**subjects**, **objects**, **predicates**, **modifiers**, **phrases**, and **clauses**). Coordinating conjunctions (*and, or,* and *nor*) form a **compound** or a list; subordinating conjunctions (such as *when, after, before, during, until, despite, although, because, if, whether, but, as*) signal that what follows is dependent on what it modifies. See **subordinate clause**.

**Consonant lineation**—a term I use to characterize a line, either **end-stopped** or **end-paused**, that honors the grammatical units of syntax; formal rhythm congruent with syntactical rhythm. James Longenbach's more elegant term (in *The Art of the Poetic Line*, Graywolf Press, 2008) is "parsing line." For contrast, see **dissonant lineation** and **enjambment**.

**Copula**—the suggestive synonym (from Latin, "a bond") for a **linking verb**, which yokes the **subject** and what is asserted about it (Frankie and Johnny *were* sweethearts).

**Couplet**—a two-line **stanza**; from the root word meaning "copulate" and bound even closer when **closed**.

**Dactyl**—in **accentual-syllabic verse**, a metrical **foot** placing a stressed syllable before two unstressed syllables *(Higgledy Piggledy)*; when repeated, a dactyl produces **falling rhythm** and **triple meter**, sometimes found hilarious.

**Definite article**—the *the*.

**Dependent clause**—another name for a **subordinate clause**.

**Diction**—the selection and use of words from the **lexicon**; generally characterized as either formal, informal, colloquial, or slang.

**Dimeter**—lines with two metrical **feet**.

**Dissonant lineation**—the opposition of rhythms in the syntax and in the line, created by a line that ends before a **phrase** is completed; an **enjambed** line, which divides (and "annotates"—see Longenbach) a coherent syntactical unit. For contrast, see **consonant lineation**, as well as **end-paused line** and **end-stopped line**.

**Duple meter**—in **accentual-syllabic verse**, an exact ratio of stressed and unstressed syllables, one of each in each **foot**; a pattern of regular **trochaic** or **iambic** feet.

**Elision**—the omission of **function words** implied by syntactical position, repeated syntactical structure, or semantic context (the one *[whom]* I love; give *[to]* him the book; the game *[being]* over, we went home).

**End-paused line**—a line that closes not with punctuation but with a natural pause in the syntax; a line that is **consonant** with a **phrase**; a line neither **end-stopped** nor **enjambed**.

**End-stopped line**—a line that closes with punctuation; a line that is wholly **consonant** with the syntax. For contrast, see **enjambment**.

**Enjambment**—a line that requires continued reading, into the next line, and sometimes (doubly suspended) into the next **stanza**, in order to complete a grammatical unit *(sticks and/stones, the quick brown/ fox, throwing/up his dinner, has been/lying, through/the* *glass darkly);* a **dissonant** line end or stanza end; the use of "artificial" rhythm whereby the formal arrangement trumps the embedded rhythms of the sentence; an "unnatural" pause in the syntax created by the white space that follows a line or stanza; a term sometimes used for any line without final punctuation, but not by me. For contrast, see **consonant lineation**, as well as **end-paused line** and **end-stopped line**.

**Falling rhythm**—in **accentual-syllabic verse**, a pattern of **feet** in which a stressed syllable is dependably followed by one or two unaccented syllables *(NOTHing conSUMES us like PROSody).* See **dactyl** and **trochee**.

**Feminine ending**—an unstressed syllable at the end of the line; a term often meaning specifically an unstressed syllable that has been added to a line of **rising rhythm**. Note: a single unstressed syllable cannot constitute a **foot**, although a single stressed syllable can.

**Figurative language**—description through analogy; specifically, simile (comparison using "like" or "as"), metaphor (substitution of one term for another), and conceit (an extended figure).

**Foot**—a unit of measure; in **accentual-syllabic verse**, a group of two or three syllables (units of sound). The position of the stressed syllable in the foot is indicated by a name derived from Greek (**iambic**, **trochaic**, **anapestic**, **dactylic**, **spondaic**, **pyrrhic**); the number of feet in the line is indicated by a Latin prefix (**di-**, **tri-**, **tetra-**, **penta-**, and **hexameter**); the two terms are combined to indicate the most prevalent foot and consistent line length (e.g., "iambic pentameter"). See **substitution** and **variant foot**.

**Form**—the coherent arrangement and relation of all the parts; in particular, the satisfying patterns, created by repetition and variation, that distinguish poems from prose, including **meter** or **cadence**, **stanzas** (with either a fixed or a varying number of lines), **anaphora**, **alliteration**, **rhyme**, **consonant** or **dissonant** lines, chiming **vowels**, recurring imagery, and other elements so arranged. Distinct from **structure** but often coincident with it.

**Function words**—replacements for **inflected** word endings (Give the ball *to* Jim; Jim is a friend *of* mine; the man *from* Mars; the man *of* La Mancha); i.e., words that contribute grammatical and not **semantic** meaning (*to* be or not *to* be); or, words that provide a rudimentary but nonsubstantive **fundament** (*It's* not for me to say).

**Fundament**—the most basic, powerful, and essential unit of **syntax**; the minimum prerequisite for a **sen-**

tence; in English, an unsubordinated **subject** and **predicate** (**verb**). Note: the subject may be elided and implied (as happens routinely in an **imperative**), but without a predicate, a group of words is grammatically incomplete and, if isolated by terminal punctuation (a period, question mark, or exclamation mark), becomes a **sentence fragment**. See **clause**.

**Gerund**—a **verb** form ending in *–ing* and used as a **noun** (*Dancing* is not allowed); distinct from a **participle**, another verb form ending in *–ing* but used as a **modifier** (Who is that *dancing* fool?) or in a **verb phrase** (They *were dancing in the hall*).

**Grammar**—a system of rules governing usage of a language.

**Half rhyme**—when either the final vowel sound or the final consonant sound, not both, is repeated in two or more words *(tame/snake; hot/cat)*; also called "slant rhyme."

**Hexameter**—lines with six metrical **feet**.

**Hypotactic syntax**—characterized by **subordinate clauses** "arranged under" *(hypo-)* the grammatically more powerful **fundament**. See **complex sentence** and, for contrast, **paratactic syntax**.

**Iamb**—in **accentual-syllabic verse**, a metrical **foot** placing a stressed syllable after an unstressed syllable *(deSIGN, comPLETE)*; produces **rising rhythm** and **duple meter** when repeated, said by some to duplicate the heartbeat.

**Imperative**—a **verb** form that expresses an address, command, or entreaty; a **sentence** using this verb form (*Eat* some beans), in which the **subject** (you) is implied rather than stated.

**Indefinite article**—*a* or *an.*

**Independent clause**—a grammatically self-sufficient and complete unit of syntax that contains at least a **predicate**, and most often a **subject** as well; can stand alone or combine with other **independent** or **subordinate clauses** to form a **sentence** (see **compound** and **complex**); needs (grammatically) no elaboration but can carry the weight of numerous less-powerful syntactical units (words, **phrases**, and **subordinate clauses**). See **fundament**.

**Infinitive**—a **verb** in its potential and most universal state, lacking specification of case, number, tense, person, or mood; can perform some functions of a **noun** (*To be* at all is *to be wrong*) or a **verb** (I wanted *to strangle* the guy, so I asked him *to leave*). Note: "to" in this formation is a **function word** and is often **elided** when the infinitive follows another verb (No one saw him *leave*, no one saw me *weep*).

**Inflection**—the changes a word may undergo to indicate case, number, tense, person, or mood *(his/ him/her, drink/drank/have drunk)*; in inflected languages, word endings that specify grammatical function (*Agnus Dei* = "lamb of God"), connect **modifiers** to their appropriate **nouns** and **verbs**, and allow for greater latitude of word placement in a sentence. Note: although a few simplified traces may be found (-*ed* for singular or plural past tense, and **pronoun** declension such as *he/him/his*), English depends instead on **function words** (lamb *of* God), the order of the words (see **natural** or **normal order** and **right-branching**), and the grouping of the **syntax** into **phrases** or functional "chunks."

**Internal rhyme**—repetition of final syllables in two or more words interior to the line(s), not solely at the ends of lines and not part of a predictable pattern. For contrast, see **rhyme scheme**.

**Interrogative**—a **verb** form that asks a question; a **sentence** using this verb form *(Can you hear me now?)*.

**Interruptive syntax**—any words or **phrase** or **dependent clause** that intrude between the parts of another syntactical unit; especially, **modifiers** separating a **subject** and **predicate** (We, *therefore, the Representatives of the united States of America, in General Congress, Assembled, appealing to the Supreme Judge of the world for the rectitude of our intentions,* do, *in the Name, and by Authority of the good People of these Colonies, solemnly* publish and declare . . .).

**Intransitive verb**—actions by the **subject** that do not "pass across" to an **object** (The wind *blew,* the rain *poured* down, and the river *rose*). See **transitive active** and **transitive passive verb**.

**Introductory syntax**—anything that precedes the **fundament** in a sentence, whether words (*Slow and lethal,* greed took over), **phrases** (*Like a thief in the house, disguised as ambition,* greed took over), or **clauses** (*Even though we'd meant to be generous,* greed took over). When the introductory material delays the fundament substantially, a **periodic sentence** is formed.

**Inverted foot**—the most common variation in **accentual-syllabic verse**, usually appearing at the beginning or the end of a line, which reverses the predominant relationship of stressed and unstressed syllables (e.g., a **trochee** in iambic **meter**, or an **iamb** in trochaic meter).

**Inverted syntax**—an arrangement of grammatical parts that reverses the **natural** or **normal** (conventional) **order** of words in a **sentence** or **clause** or **phrase**; common in **interrogatives** *(Are you happy yet?),* resisted as "poetic" when intended to elevate the perception *(Fleet was her foot, and saddened was I then).*

**Lexicon**—vocabulary; the collection of words in a language.

**Linking verb**—an **intransitive** assertion of existence or emotion (We *are* jerks and we *feel* awful); some form of *be, become, feel, look, seem,* or *appear;* the least active **predicate**.

**Masculine ending**—a stressed syllable at the end of the line.

**Masculine rhyme**—repetition of sounds occurring in monosyllabic words (*cat* in a *hat*) or in final syllables that are stressed (*unLESS/conFESS,* but not *SISter/ BROTHer*).

**Meter**—literally, a "measure": in music, the mathematical system governing relative time values for each note, a source of ongoing pulse, and the basis for variations that create rhythm; in poetry, an established pattern that regularizes the number of syllables in each line, or the number of stresses, or both, to organize and foreground the many variations of rhythm, pitch, and duration inherent in the language. See **accentual, accentual-syllabic**, and **syllabic verse**.

**Modifier**—an **adjective, adverb, article, noun, participal, phrase**, or **restrictive clause** used as a defining adjunct to another word; syntactically weak because grammatically dependent, but descriptively powerful because able to limit, expand, or contradict the consensual meaning of a **noun** or **verb**.

**Natural** or **normal order**—the most straightforward syntactical structure in English, placing the **fundament** first in the **sentence** (**subject**, then **predicate** and optional **object**), with any elaboration kept subsequent to it. For contrast, see **interruptive, introductory, inverted**, and **periodic syntax**.

**Noun**—the name of a person, place, thing, or idea; can serve as the **subject** of a verb, as the **object** of a **verb** or **preposition**, and even as an **adjective** (the *water* bucket).

**Noun phrase**—a unit of **syntax** incorporating a **noun** and all its **modifiers**, including **adjectival phrases** or **clauses**; or, any group of words—including a **clause**—

that serves the function of a **subject** or **object** in a sentence (*Kissing the cook* will get you second helpings; *We are happy* is our mantra; See *how they run*).

**Object**—a **noun** or **noun phrase** that receives the action of a **verb** (You can't always get *what you want*) or a **preposition** (in this *world*).

**Open couplet**—a two-line **stanza** that does not coincide with the structure of the syntax—i.e., the **sentence** or **clause** or **phrase** continues beyond the unpunctuated end of the second line. See **enjambment**.

**Parallel syntax**—repetition of the same grammatical unit *(to form a more perfect Union, establish Justice, insure domestic Tranquility, provide for the common defence, promote the general Welfare, and secure the Blessings of Liberty).*

**Paratactic syntax**—a **sentence** or series of sentences aligning **independent clauses** of equal *(para-)* syntactical power *(I came, I saw, I conquered)*; sometimes connected by coordinating **conjunctions**, such as *and* (see fiction by Ernest Hemingway). See **compound sentence** and **hypotactic syntax**.

**Participle**—a verb form that functions in the syntax as a **modifier**; employs *-ing* or *-ed*, or an irregular past tense or **transitive passive** conjugation (e.g., *thrown*); may, if **transitive**, take an **object**, forming a participial **phrase** (the person *pouring the coffee*).

**Pentameter**—lines with five metrical **feet**.

**Periodic sentence**—when the **fundament** is significantly delayed by phrases and/or clauses (*When in the Course of human events, it becomes necessary for one people to dissolve the political bands which have connected them with another, and to assume among the powers of the earth, the separate and equal station to which the Laws of Nature and of Nature's God entitle them, a decent respect to the opinions of mankind requires . . .*).

**Phrase**—in music, a unit of rhythm or melody that recurs and combines with other phrases to create a musical structure; in **syntax**, a coherent but dependent group of words that combines with other phrases and a **fundament** to create a **sentence**; in **grammar**, a cluster of words containing a functional part of speech and its **modifiers**, less powerful than a **clause** because lacking its own **predicate**. See **adjectival**, **adverbial**, **noun**, **participial**, **prepositional**, and **verb phrases**.

**Predicate**—a **verb** or **verb phrase** that contains the central action committed or received by the **subject**; the irreducible **fundament** of English syntax and the engine of the **sentence**; the essential part of a logical proposition.

**Preposition**—a word that combines with an **object** (a **noun** or **pronoun**) to specify relative context in space, time, or argument (such as *in, on, toward, under, over, above, around, through, beyond, behind, before, after, despite, to, of, from, about*); in uninflected languages, a **function word**.

**Prepositional phrase**—a unit of **grammar** yoking a **preposition** to an **object** and its descriptive adjuncts; used to **modify** a **noun** (the wind *in the willows*) or a **verb** (The storm was stalled *along the rocky coast*); frequently appears in both **parallel** and **right-branching syntax**.

**Pronoun**—a substitute for a **noun** *(he/she/we/they, you/me/us/them, this/that/these/those, who/whose/ what/which, one/any/some/most)* or **noun phrase** (The president delivered a plan for the future, and *it* was appalling).

**Pyrrhic foot**—in **accentual-syllabic verse**, a **variant** metrical unit consisting of two unstressed syllables *(of the, -ingly)*. Like a Pyrrhic victory, it achieves the goal (preservation of metrical pattern) but at excessive cost (no **cadence**-producing stresses).

**Quatrain**—a four-line **stanza**.

**Restrictive clause**—a group of words containing a **subject** and **predicate** that provides necessary **modification** of a word or phrase and limits its meaning (The coffee *[that] I ordered* was cold; The person *who poured it* was an idiot); characterized in American usage by *that,* not *which* (which indicates additional but not required qualification); a species of **subordinate clause**, with the subordinating pronouns *(that, who, whom)* often elided.

**Rhyme**—repetition of the final consonant and vowel sounds in the final syllables of two or more words (The c*at* is named Jehoso*phat*). For contrast, see **half rhyme**.

**Rhyme scheme**—a pattern of **rhyme** at the ends of proximate lines, notated by assigning a new letter to each new sound (abba, bccb, efga, etc.). For contrast, see **internal rhyme**.

**Right-branching syntax**—when modification follows in closest proximity to what is **modified**; usually, elaboration extending from the "trunk" of the **fundament** *(I pledge allegiance / to the flag / of the United States / of America)*. For contrast, see **parallel syntax**.

**Rising rhythm**—in **accentual-syllabic verse**, a pattern of **feet** in which a stressed syllable dependably follows one or two unaccented syllables. See **iamb** and **anapest**.

**Semantic**—of or related to meaning derived from words.

**Sentence**—a distinct, grammatically independent utterance, usually marked by a period, question mark, or exclamation mark at its completion; must contain at least one **independent clause**, thereby expressing a complete syntactical thought; in English, must contain a **predicate** (**verb**). See **fundament**.

**Sentence fragment**—a distinct utterance, marked by concluding punctuation, that lacks a **predicate**; an incomplete syntactical thought.

**Simple declarative sentence**—the most basic English **sentence** structure; contains only one **clause**, which must be **independent**. See **complex** and **compound sentences** for alternative structures.

**Sonnet**—a poem of fourteen lines, **structured** to examine paradox; conventionally, in **iambic pentameter** with a **rhyme scheme** that reinforces its argument: in the Petrarchan sonnet, a premise established in the *octave* (eight lines) in interlocking quatrains (abbaabba) is contradicted in the *sestet* (six lines) in a new set of rhyming sounds (e.g., cdecde); in the Shakespearean sonnet, **quatrains** (abab cdcd efef) are responded to in a final **closed couplet** (gg). The sonnet's *volta*, or "turn," usually at line 9 or line 13, has become an inherent expectation for most short lyric poems.

**Spondee**—in **accentual-syllabic verse**, a **variant** metrical **foot** joining two stressed syllables *(woodchuck, blackboard, heartbreak, blind mice, deep peace)*; increases the ratio of stressed to unstressed syllables in the line.

**Stanza**—from the Italian for "room"; a group of lines clustered together, and separated from the other lines, by white space, which enforces a pause; a formal arrangement that may be regular (same number of lines in each) or irregular, **closed** (ending in punctuation), or **open**; sometimes called a "verse paragraph," especially when coincident with the **structure** of the poem.

**Structure**—the order in which information is released to the reader; a purposeful organization of the materials. Distinct from **form** but often coincident with it. See Voigt, *The Flexible Lyric* (University of Georgia Press, 1999) or Stephen Dobyns, *Best Words, Best Order* (St. Martin's Press, 2003).

**Subject**—a **noun** or **noun phrase** on which something is predicated; in a **clause**, that which initiates or receives an action or assertion (*Nothing* is wrong; *Slow and steady* wins the race); half the **fundament** of the **sentence**.

**Subjunctive**—a "mood" controlling the conjugation of **verbs**, expressive of the conditional and merely possible (If I *were* rich, I *would live* in Paris) rather than assertive of fact.

**Subordinate clause**—a group of words containing its own **subject** and **predicate** but unable to function independently as the **fundament** of a sentence; expresses a substantive but incomplete thought; usually marked by a subordinating **conjunction** or **pronoun** *(after we left; who wanted to leave),* but this marker may be elided (we lost the dog *[that] we adored*); most often used to modify a **noun** (the dog *we adored*) or a **verb** (bit the mailman *each time he came to the door*); may take the function of a noun (*What you see* is *what you* *get*); may introduce, follow, or interrupt an **independent clause** to form a **complex sentence**. See also **hypotactic syntax**, **periodic syntax**, and **restrictive clause**.

**Substitution**—in **accentual-syllabic meter**, the common replacement of the dominant **foot** with a unit containing a different relationship of stressed to unstressed syllables (e.g., an **iamb** in a line of **falling rhythm**), or a different number of syllables (e.g., an **anapest** in a line of **duple meter**). See **inverted foot**, **pyrrhic foot**, **spondee**, and **variant foot**.

**Syllabic verse**—poetic **meter** devised by a fixed number of syllables in every line, whether they are stressed or unstressed. Note: in English, which depends on the location of stress (a rise in pitch or increased duration) for denotative meaning, syllabic patterns are essentially unheard and therefore not a true rhythmic system; nonetheless, they strengthen the artifice of the line over syntactical **cadence** to suggest a formal regularity in composition.

**Syntax**—the order of the words in a sentence.

**Tercet**—a three-line **stanza**.

**Tetrameter**—lines with four metrical **feet**.

**Transitive active verb**—an action, by the **subject** of the **sentence** or **clause**, that "passes across" to an **object** (I *saw* a cat and *said* hello, which *caused* him to panic).

**Transitive passive verb**—an action redirected back to the **subject** of the **sentence** or **clause** (The cat *was greeted* warmly; the panic *was caused* by neurosis).

**Trimeter**—lines with three metrical **feet**.

**Triple meter**—in **accentual-syllabic verse**, created when two unstressed syllables appear with regularity before (**anapestic**) or after (**dactylic**) every stressed syllable. Said to "gallop."

**Trochee**—in **accentual-syllabic verse**, a metrical **foot** in which a stressed syllable is placed before an unstressed syllable *(WILLiam FAULKner),* creating **falling rhythm** and **duple meter** when repeated.

**Variant foot**—an exception to the dominant pattern of the chosen poetic **meter**; crucial employment of variation to avoid tedium and introduce effective rhythm. The most common examples (1) maintain the same number of syllables with a new position for the stress among them (**inverted foot**); (2) maintain the position of the stress (first or last, for **falling** or **rising rhythm**) but add or subtract an unstressed syllable; or (3) **substitute** a stressed or unstressed syllable for its opposite to create a **spondee** or **pyrrhic foot**.

**Verb**—a word expressing an action, an occurrence, or a mode of being; as a **predicate**, the essential half of the **fundament** and the grammatical center of a **sentence** or a **clause**; in its various conjugations, the primary and most economical means for management of time, and thus crucial to narrative. See **intransitive**, **linking**, **transitive active**, and **transitive passive verbs**.

**Verb phrase**—a unit of **syntax** containing a **verb**, its (optional) **object**, and all **modifiers**, including **adverbs**, **adverbial phrases**, **participial phrases**, **prepositional phrases**, and **subordinate clauses** (*Now* we *are engaged in a great civil war, testing whether that nation, or any nation, so conceived and so dedicated, can long endure*).

**Vowels**—one of the two sets of speech sounds from which the **lexicon** is formed, and the only one (a) that may stand alone to create a syllable or a word, and (b) in which breath is not constricted enough to create friction. "Long" vowel sounds have the greatest degree of openness and thereby usually receive durational stress; in poetry, they provide a source of emotive and connotative values, as well as sensual, musical pleasure—the *ay* in *flame* and *break, weigh* and *grey;* the *ah* in *dark* and *dawn, talk* and *taut;* the *ee* in *meat* and *mete, key* and *conceive;* the *eye* in *why* and *buy, mice* and *height;* the *oh* in *so* and *sew* and *sow,* in *bone* and *boat* and *beau,* in *gauche* and *dough;* the *ooh* in *balloon* and *ruthless* and *route;* the *yew* in *puke* and *beauty.*

# Acknowledgments

Portions of this study were previously published, in other versions, in the *Kenyon Review,* as "Syntax: Rhythm of Thought, Rhythm of Song" (vol. 25, no. 1: Winter 2003) and "On and Off the Grid: Syntax Part II" (vol. 26, no. 3: Summer 2004). "On and Off the Grid" was reprinted in *Poet's Work, Poet's Play: Essays on the Practice and the Art,* Daniel Tobin and Pimone Triplett, eds. (University of Michigan Press, 2008).

All quotations from Robert Jourdain are taken from his book *Music, the Brain, and Ecstasy* (Morrow, 1997). Stories by Maeve Brennan can be found in *The Springs of Affection* (Houghton Mifflin, 1997). The most accessible introduction to neurolinguistics is Steven Pinker's *The Language Instinct* (HarperCollins, 1995).

Thanks to the Rockefeller Foundation for my residency at Bellagio, where I began the first articulation of this book. Thanks to Charlie Baxter, for dreaming up *The Art of . . .* series at Graywolf Press and conscripting me for syntax. And special thanks to the MFA Program for Writers at Warren Wilson College, where I tried out most of my thinking about this material in classes and lectures. My colleagues' generous, sharp-witted responses to those presentations, and to drafts of these pages, were invaluable.

## Permission Acknowledgments

**ELLEN BRYANT VOIGT** is the author of seven collections of poetry, including *Messenger: New and Selected Poems 1976–2006,* which was a finalist for the National Book Award and the Pulitzer Prize. She is the author of a collection of essays on poetry and craft, *The Flexible Lyric.* She has received the Fellowship from the Academy of American Poets and the O. B. Hardison, Jr. Poetry Prize, and she served as Vermont State Poet from 1999 to 2003. She is currently a chancellor of the Academy of American Poets. Voigt founded and teaches in the writing program at Warren Wilson College. She lives in Cabot, Vermont.

This book is made possible through a partnership with the College of Saint Benedict, and honors the legacy of S. Mariella Gable, a distinguished teacher at the College.

Other titles in this series include:

*Loverboy* by Victoria Redel

*The House on Eccles Road* by Judith Kitchen

*One Vacant Chair* by Joe Coomer

*The Weatherman* by Clint McCown

*Collected Poems* by Jane Kenyon

*Variations on the Theme of an African Dictatorship* by Nuruddin Farah:

    *Sweet and Sour Milk*

    *Sardines*

    *Close Sesame*

*Duende* by Tracy K. Smith

*All of It Singing: New and Selected Poems* by Linda Gregg

*How to Escape from a Leper Colony* by Tiphanie Yanique

*One Day I Will Write About This Place* by Binyavanga Wainaina

*The Convert: A Tale of Exile and Extremism* by Deborah Baker

*On Sal Mal Lane* by Ru Freeman

Support for this series has been provided by the Manitou Fund as part of the Warner Reading Program.

The text of *The Art of Syntax: Rhythm of Thought, Rhythm of Song* is set in Warnock Pro, a typeface designed by Robert Slimbach for Adobe Systems in 2000. Book design by Wendy Holdman. Composition by BookMobile Design and Publishing Services, Minneapolis, Minnesota. Manufactured by Versa Press on acid-free paper.